Effectively Managing
Troublesome Employees

EFFECTIVELY MANAGING TROUBLESOME EMPLOYEES

R. Bruce McAfee
Paul J. Champagne

QUORUM BOOKS
Westport, Connecticut • London

Library of Congress Cataloging-in-Publication Data

McAfee, R. Bruce.
  Effectively managing troublesome employees / R. Bruce McAfee, Paul
J. Champagne.
    p. cm.
  Includes bibliographical references.
  ISBN 0–89930–773–6 (alk. paper)
  1. Problem employees. 2. Labor discipline. 3. Supervision of
employees. I. Champagne, Paul J.
  HF5549.5.E42M3 1994
  658.3'045—dc20   93–49029

British Library Cataloguing in Publication Data is available.

Library of Congress Catalog Card Number: 93–49029
ISBN: 0–89930–773–6

First published in 1994

Quorum Books, 88 Post Road West, Westport, CT 06881
An imprint of Greenwood Publishing Group, Inc.

Printed in the United States of America

The paper used in this book complies with the
Permanent Paper Standard issued by the National
Information Standards Organization (Z39.48–1984).

10 9 8 7 6 5 4 3 2 1

Contents

Preface

In the course of a typical workday, managers and supervisors are periodically confronted with employee behavior that is either potentially or clearly disruptive. Solving these problems becomes a top priority, but in many cases managers do not know how to proceed or what options are available. What can they do without creating a basis for legal action by the employee? How should they proceed in order to reduce the risk of a grievance? What general principles should guide their actions so the behavior problem is resolved?

The purpose of this book is to address and answer the questions just raised. It attempts to provide managers with current and specific information regarding troublesome employees. The overriding consideration is to constructively resolve problem situations that affect any organization. Each chapter discusses a different aspect of the disciplinary process or a type of disruptive behavior and describes what a manager can and cannot do in order to deal with the employees involved.

The book is intended for managers in many different kinds of union and nonunion organizations. We have tried to reflect this broad orientation in both the presentation of materials and the various company examples cited.

We are grateful for the assistance provided by the editorial and production staffs at Quorum Books. We are especially grateful to Patricia McClenney for her invaluable assistance in preparing the manuscript for publication.

Effectively Managing
Troublesome Employees

Chapter 1

Principles for Effective Discipline

Because he was late to work one day, Larry parked on the city street next to the firm's office building. This parking area was not owned by the company, but it had been unwritten practice for only managerial personnel and customers to park there. A large parking lot next to the building was designated for employees. That day Larry's supervisor confronted him and told him to stop parking on the street. Larry argued that he had just as much right to park there as anyone else. A week later, Larry again used the area to park when he was late and the supervisor observed it. Suppose that you are the supervisor; what would you do in this case?

As this incident demonstrates, managers are often confronted with complex and difficult decisions regarding disciplinary issues. Should Larry be disciplined or should his behavior be ignored? A good case can be made for either choice.

In this opening chapter, we examine a variety of issues related to discipline. These include the pros and cons of using punishment, how penalties can best be administered, and the differences between two major disciplinary systems. Finally, we discuss seven basic principles related to what constitutes fair play when taking disciplinary action.

PUNISHMENT: SHOULD A MANAGER USE IT?

"Punishment" is typically thought of as an aversive event that follows an employee's behavior and decreases the frequency of that behavior. For example, an employee who is tardy (behavior) might be given a written reprimand (punishment). Assuming that the employee dislikes reprimands, the frequency of tardiness should decrease. A second form of punishment occurs when a manager withdraws something valued by the employee as a result of that person's behavior. For example, a manager may withhold a raise because the employee has been excessively tardy.

In comparison, "discipline" has three basic meanings: (1) training that molds, strengthens, improves, or corrects; (2) control gained by enforced obedience; and (3) punishment for violations of rules, standards, and direct orders.[1] In other words, discipline has both a training and an education aspect as well as an enforcement and punishment side. The former is preventive and concentrates on gaining voluntary support for necessary rules and regulations, whereas the latter is corrective and aims at eliminating the unwanted behavior in the future.

Given these definitions, should managers and organizations use punishment and take corrective disciplinary action against employees? Many people have argued that punishment should be avoided as a means of influencing behavior. They contend that discipline can cause anxiety in the person disciplined and, for that matter, in the person delivering the discipline. The former's anxiety can result in hostility toward the person administering the discipline (the supervisor), which in turn can lead to attempts to "get even" later (e.g., sabotage or restricting output). In addition, the hostility may cause employees to use their creative abilities to figure out ways to break the rules without incurring disciplinary action.

The fear associated with discipline/punishment may lead the employee to avoid the manager, making it more difficult to monitor that employee's job performance and possibly improve it. Fear of being punished may also encourage employees to hide errors. Factory workers might put a small damaged tool into their lunchbox or throw it into the trash rather than report the damage. Expensive monitoring and surveillance may be necessary in such cases.

Critics also contend that the fear of punishment can cause rigidity in behavior. Employees may become hesitant to do anything without first obtaining the supervisor's approval. In some cases this may be beneficial to an organization, but it can also result in reduced initiative and creativity among employees.

Finally, some critics argue that punishment never really eliminates undesirable behavior but only temporarily suppresses it. These behaviors will recur once the threat of punishment is removed or will reappear in different situations, perhaps in a somewhat modified form.

Although critics cite many arguments against the use of punishment, others maintain that it has some important advantages. Unlike other motivational strategies, the use of penalties has the potential to rapidly change an employee's behavior. When employees engage in totally unacceptable behaviors such as violating important safety rules, damaging company property, or fighting, quick behavioral change is often necessary. Disciplinary action may be the only potentially effective strategy in these situations.[2]

In addition to being relatively quick, penalties are often inexpensive. It costs little or nothing to give an employee a verbal or written warning. Even suspensions are usually quite inexpensive, because employees are typically not paid during the suspension period. It is important to add that setting up a disciplinary system and communicating it to all employees does involve some initial expense. However, this one-time cost is usually not very high.

Advocates of the use of punishment argue that it is a natural part of our life. We learn not to run on ice, drive too fast around curves, or wear light clothing in the winter, all because nature punishes us. Furthermore, nature changes our behavior without causing any long-term emotional damage or neuroses. Advocates conclude that because punishment is a natural occurrence, its use does not have to result in adverse consequences for either the employee or the organization.

Finally, some suggest that punishment is the only feasible strategy one can use to change behaviors that are themselves rewarding.[3] For example, if an employee goes to sleep on the job, sleeping is its own reinforcer. To change the behavior, some consequence must be used to offset the reward provided by the behavior. Punishment is typically the only feasible and equitable consequence in these situations.

It is important that managers be aware of the potential disadvantages of punishment. By the same token, punishment or the threat of it seems to be the only feasible, equitable, or economically justifiable approach a manager can use in some situations. The critical question is not whether to use punishment, but when and how it should be implemented.

HOW SHOULD PUNISHMENT BE ADMINISTERED?

The "hot stove" rules offer a good analogy to guide one's disciplinary practices.[4] A stove is clearly one of the most necessary and useful appliances in any home. It is a source of good food and helps remove the chill on a frosty morning. There is only one simple rule: "Don't touch." The stove is a powerful teacher because it takes only one touch for someone to learn that when it is hot it should be avoided. It causes behavior to change immediately and permanently. The stove is also a consistent teacher. It will deliver its lesson to anybody at any time; there is no discrimination.

The stove accomplishes this without causing damaging emotional reactions. Few would harbor any resentment or hatred toward the stove even though they may be burned. How does the stove change behavior so effectively and yet not create resentment, anger, or hostility? Contained in the answer to this question are the principles of an effective disciplinary policy and the best use of penalties.

Punish Immediately

The effect of punishment is enhanced when the manager disciplines as soon as possible after undesired behavior occurs. If employees are to change their behavior, they need rapid feedback that allows them to clearly associate the disciplinary stimulus with the inappropriate behavior. The longer the time between the unacceptable behavior and its consequences, the less likely the employee will associate the two.[5]

There is another important reason why discipline should be immediate. Because employees typically work in groups, the behavior of one person is observed by many others. If someone engages in an inappropriate behavior (e.g., fails to wear safety glasses, smokes in unauthorized places, or arrives at work late) and the manager appears to be taking no action, other employees may conclude that the behavior is acceptable or that the organization is not consistently enforcing its rules. In addition, the other employees may respond by "testing the limits" of the rules.

Another risk associated with the use of delayed discipline is that rule violators may continue their inappropriate behavior and thereby lead to dysfunctional consequences for the organization, the employee, or both. For example, construction workers who work without hard hats once and are not disciplined immediately may continue to do so and ultimately suffer an injury. Likewise, an employee who is not disciplined immediately for stealing company property may continue to steal until some action is taken.

Penalize Consistently

It is recommended that managers administer penalties consistently. The penalty given for a specific offense today should be the same as the one given tomorrow, next week, next month, or next year (assuming the rules do not change). In addition, all employees should be disciplined equally; prejudice, bias, and favoritism should not enter into the process.

A frequent question is whether or not extenuating circumstances should be taken into account. For example, suppose two workers are both seen without hard hats in a restricted area. One has thirty years' seniority, a spotless record, and is considered one of the best employees in the company. The second is new and is a marginal performer. If the company has a policy that workers who fail to wear hard hats in designated areas will be suspended for three days, should both employees receive equal penalties? Should the superior worker be given special consideration because of his or her work record?

One could argue that if an organization considers any extenuating circumstances when administering penalties, it contradicts the idea of consistency. On the other hand, if an organization always considers these factors and does so uniformly at all times and for all people, it would not necessarily be violating the consistency principle.

At least one study has suggested that managers should be consistent in yet another way: they should administer those penalties prescribed by the firm's disciplinary policy. In this study the researcher analyzed the personnel records of 150 employees: fifty employees had been penalized according to the policy and the penalty remained a permanent part of their record; fifty had been penalized but in a manner not consistent with the policy and/or subsequently had the penalty removed from their record; and fifty had broken the organizational rule regarding absenteeism but had not received any penalty. The results showed that absenteeism over the subsequent twenty-month period was lowest for the group of employees who had been penalized in accordance with company policy.[6]

Penalize Actions, Not Personality

Punishment is most effective when it is dispensed in an impersonal manner whereby the focus is on the act itself.[7] This does not mean that it must be done in writing, nor does it imply that a manager should express no personal feelings whatsoever when disciplining the employee. "Impersonal" means that a manager should discipline workers in private whenever possible and focus on the employee's behavior and its consequences, rather than on the individual's personality. When an employee engages in an inappropriate action, a manager may be tempted to get angry and say something like, "You are a complete idiot for doing that!" or "You are totally irresponsible." Although such statements may seem warranted at that moment, generalizations about someone's personality can cause that person to become angry and defensive, which is not conducive to rational understanding or effective behavioral change. Discussions of a specific behavior are considerably less threatening and are more likely to provide a clear understanding of the supervisor's expectations. For example:

Poor:	What is the matter with you? Don't you know that those reports have to be done correctly the first time?
Better:	When you don't complete sales reports accurately, shipments of your orders are delayed. This costs us money, and it costs you money.
Poor:	You are totally irresponsible. It's absurd that you are late so often. Shape up!
Better:	I see that you're late again. When this happens it really delays others from completing their work and slows customer service.

Provide a Rationale

Punishment is more effective if managers provide a clear, unambiguous reason for it; tell the employee how to avoid further penalties; and explain what the consequences will be if the employee continues to behave inappropriately.[8] Administering discipline immediately, consistently, and impersonally has some informational value, but the information such action provides is often not clear.

Some large organizations now require managers to provide this information in writing. These organizations often stress the importance of making sure employees know the consequences of further deviant behavior.

Establish a Supportive Relationship

Should a manager administering punishment have a relatively close and warm relationship with the employee being punished, or should the relationship be cold and distant? Evidence indicates that penalties work best when they are delivered within the context of a warm and friendly relationship, because subordinates are more apt to accept a penalty and change their behavior if the supervisor has helped them develop their skills and abilities and has often rewarded and been supportive of them.

In some organizations, managers and employees have developed tremendous animosity over the years. Ideally, managers in these situations should attempt to gradually improve the relationships. In the interim, however, they still need to administer penalties in a less-than-ideal atmosphere and prepare themselves for one or more negative side effects of discipline.

DOES DISCIPLINE CHANGE EMPLOYEE BEHAVIOR AND ATTITUDES?

Despite the fact that nearly all companies commonly use penalties such as verbal warnings, written warnings, suspensions, and threats of firing, relatively little empirical evidence of their effectiveness is available. Fortunately, some research has addressed two topics of particular importance to managers: (1) Does punishment or the threat of it change employee behavior or satisfaction? (2) How can or should punishment be given to increase the probability that it will be successful?

A few studies have considered whether discipline actually changes employee behavior or attitudes and, if so, in what ways. One of these investigated whether threatening to fine employees for cash register shortages would reduce theft or carelessness. Six cashiers at a small twelve-hour-a-day, seven-day-a-week restaurant served as subjects. The following procedure was used: if any single day's cash shortage equaled or exceeded 1 percent of that day's sales receipts, the total shortage, divided by the number of cashiers working that day, was subtracted from each cashier's pay. The investigation ran for forty-one days and was divided into four periods. During the first period, which lasted five days, the investigators found that the cash register was short on all five days for a total of 4.02 percent of sales. In the remaining three periods, the fines were instituted for twelve days (Period 2), rescinded for three days (Period 3), and reinstituted for twenty-one days (Period 4). There was a drastic reduction in shortage during the days when the threat of a fine was in effect. During Period 3, when the threat of fines was removed, shortages occurred on all three days and averaged 4.16 percent of sales.[9]

Although this study could be criticized for its small sample size and short duration, it demonstrates that the threat of penalties can change employee behavior. Note that in the study no cashier was actually fined. It was the threat rather than fines per se that changed the cashiers' behavior.

In contrast, other researchers have investigated situations in which employees were in fact penalized. One study involved nineteen locations of a large, unnamed U.S. corporation that manufactures, sells, installs, and services a wide range of products within a single industry. The researchers systematically interviewed 153 supervisors who had each referred subordinates with a drinking problem. In addition, 321 other managers were interviewed about how they managed a problem employee. Managers were asked to state the types of disciplinary actions that had been taken and what effect they had on employee behavior. In addition, they were asked to describe the topics covered in informal discussions with problem employees. Included were the constructive topics discussed (e.g., employee's explanations of own work performance, counseling services available, and other ways to get help) and the number of confrontational topics reviewed (e.g., possible disciplinary steps, employee's poor job performance, and the likely effects of poor performance on the employee's work record). The researchers found that the use of constructive topics in informal discussions had positive effects on subsequent employee job performance, whereas confrontational topics had negative outcomes. Suspending employees for a short period of time was found to improve performance, but written warnings and longer suspensions were counterproductive.[10] This study provides evidence that disciplinary action does indeed affect employee behavior, but not necessarily in a positive way. Whether managers are successful in changing employee behavior seems to depend on the approach they take and the severity of the penalty. The study suggests that managers would be wise to take a counseling, problem-solving approach rather than a punitive one.

The study just described focused on the effects of disciplining employees on their subsequent behavior; another study examined whether, and in what ways, discipline has an impact on employee attitudes toward supervision. Researchers surveyed 526 hourly employees in an oil refinery about disciplinary topics and attitudes toward their supervisors. They found that the supervisors' disciplining behavior was highly correlated with employee feelings. More specifically, the researchers suggested that worker dissatisfaction was highest when supervisors were abusive in disciplining employees, were inconsistent in their application of discipline, were apt to use informal punishers, and did not support their employees. The study also found that supervisory disciplinary behaviors had relatively low correlations with the employees' overall job satisfaction.[11]

This study is important because it suggests that the manner in which supervisors discipline employees can affect the subordinates' attitudes toward them. Whereas the previous study suggests that a confrontational approach is often counterproductive in terms of improving the employee's job performance, this one seems to indicate that such an approach may also result in negative attitudes toward the supervisor.

DISCIPLINARY SYSTEMS

By far the most common approach to discipline in use today is a progressive penalty system. However, there are other options for a firm to consider, including the "discipline without punishment" approach. In this section we consider the essential features of these two generic systems.

Progressive Penalty System

Any progressive penalty system is based on the premise that employee behavior can be changed through the application of ever-increasing degrees of punishment. The system consists of a series of steps, one or more of which can be eliminated or added. Most organizations have between three and five steps. Exhibit 1.1 presents an example of a progressive penalty system used by a large construction organization. Typically, when employees violate a rule they are warned verbally and told that if the infraction occurs again within a specific period, they will receive a more severe penalty. If employees then commit the same or similar violation, they are given a written warning, a copy of which is placed in their personnel file. They may be asked to sign the written warning, which serves as proof that they have been warned. Employees are told that repeated misconduct will be disciplined again, but more severely. If employees again transgress, they are suspended without pay and are warned that one more infraction will result in discharge. Finally, after one more rule infraction, employees are terminated.

Many organizations that use the progressive penalty system differentiate between serious or major offenses and less serious or minor offenses. Serious offenses (e.g., theft, gross insubordination, assault, fighting, and dishonesty) usually result in termination or suspension on the first offense;

Exhibit 1.1
Example of Progressive Disciplinary System From a Large
Construction Company

1. PURPOSE: The purpose of this disciplinary policy is to set forth principles and guidelines designed to achieve fair and consistent treatment of employees in disciplinary matters. In all but serious offenses, the organization will follow a progressive disciplinary policy designed to correct behavior or attitudes which are not acceptable in a work environment.

2. TYPES OF OFFENSES: Offenses by employees are of two general classes:

   A. SERIOUS OFFENSES: Serious offenses are offenses which justify a termination or suspension without prior verbal or written warnings or other attempts to correct the conduct of the employee involved. Serious offenses are of the type set forth in paragraph three below.

   B. LESS SERIOUS OFFENSES: Less serious offenses are offenses which do not call for termination of an employee for the first offense but for milder forms of discipline aimed at correcting the improper conduct of employees. Less serious offenses are of the type set forth in paragraph four below.

3. SERIOUS OFFENSES: The following offenses are of the type which are considered serious offenses which justify termination for the first offense. The following are for purposes of illustration and are not considered to be all-inclusive; theft or mishandling of monies, deliberate falsification of records, refusal to follow a direct order, use of drugs or intoxicants on company property, immoral conduct, assault, dishonesty, insubordination, and gross negligence.

4. LESS SERIOUS OFFENSES: The following offenses are of the type which are considered less serious offenses. In disciplining employees for less serious offenses, progressive disciplinary procedures set forth in paragraph 5 are to be followed. The following are for purposes of illustration and are not to be considered all-inclusive: absenteeism, leaving the work site without permission, failure to be physically present at work site, failure to notify the supervisor of an absence, tardiness, horseplay, and failure to turn in required reports on time.

5. PROGRESSIVE DISCIPLINARY PROCEDURE: In disciplining an employee for less serious offenses, the following sequence will take place: a) First offense, Verbal warning; b) Second offense, Written warning; c) Third offense, Suspension; d) Fourth offense, Termination.

   No two cases are ever alike and the progressive disciplinary path will vary from case to case. The steps set forth above are a suggested norm.

6. REVIEW PROCEDURE: Any employee who wishes to contest disciplinary action must comply with the following procedure:

   STEP ONE: The employee first must discuss the matter with the immediate supervisor.

   STEP TWO: If the matter is not resolved under Step One, the employee may file a written grievance with the immediate supervisor within five (5) working days of the date of the event or the occurrence giving rise to the grievance. Such written grievance shall be on forms provided by the supervisor and shall

Exhibit 1.1 (continued)

describe the facts surrounding the grievance and set forth the relief desired. The supervisor shall answer the grievance in writing.

STEP THREE: If the matter is not resolved under Step Two, the employee may, within three (3) working days after receipt of the supervisor's written answer, request that the matter be appealed to the President. The decision of the President will be final and binding on all concerned.

---

the first two steps (verbal and written warning) are skipped. Minor offenses (e.g., tardiness, horseplay, and leaving the work site without permission) usually result in a verbal warning on the first transgression. No steps are skipped when further violations occur.

Discipline without Punishment

An alternative to the traditional progressive penalty system is "discipline without punishment." First used at a Douglas fir plywood mill, its most unique feature is the attempt not to use "punishment." The procedure itself consists of sequential steps that managers follow when an employee breaks a rule:

Step 1: The manager offers the worker a casual and friendly reminder on the job that a work rule has been broken.

Step 2: Upon a second rule violation, the manager again calls attention to the violation, usually on the job, and in addition explains the need for the rule. At this time the manager makes sure the worker understands the explanation.

Step 3: In the event of another violation, Step 2 is repeated with a few modifications. The manager's boss is also present during the discussion. The employee is told that if the work or work rule is distasteful, perhaps he or she should seek another job. The employee is told that vocational counseling is available through the personnel office. The conversation is confirmed in a letter sent to the employee's home.

Step 4: Following the next rule violation within six to eight weeks of Step 3, the manager and his or her boss meet again with the employee. The employee is directed to go home for the rest of the day and decide between abiding by the company rules or quitting. The employee is paid for the time at home and is told that another violation will lead to termination.

Step 5: Upon return to work, the employee is asked for his/her decision. If the employee's decision is to abide by the rules, he or she returns to work. If a further incident occurs within six to eight weeks, the employee is terminated.

If several incidents occur within a short time, the company may skip Steps 2 and 3. If criminal behavior or fighting occurs within the plant, the employee is terminated immediately.

Several hundred companies have used a similar system, including Union Carbide; Fraser Mills (British Columbia), a division of Crown-Zellerbach; General Electric's Meter Business Department; Liberty National Bank (Oklahoma); Tampa Electric; the Texas Department of Mental Health and Mental Retardation; and General Telephone.

What are the results of discipline without punishment? Union Carbide reports that discipline without punishment has resulted in reduced absenteeism, turnover, and disciplinary actions at ten locations. Data generated from employee attitude surveys conducted before and after the implementation of discipline without punishment showed improvement in several areas. Employee perceptions of the quality of their relationship with immediate or near-immediate supervisors improved; general morale increased; and quality of communication improved. In addition, the firm believes it is in a better position to defend itself against wrongful termination suits as a result of using this approach. It makes it harder for employees to say they didn't understand the rules, and employees have the choice of quitting or staying and abiding by the rules.[12]

At Liberty National Bank, the discipline without punishment approach reduced absenteeism, turnover, and disciplinary problems. There was a noticeable improvement in morale and greater supervisory self-confidence in confronting employee problems. Exposure to equal opportunity complaints or lawsuits resulting from unfair or inconsistent disciplinary action was reduced.[13]

Tampa Electric reports the discipline without punishment has resulted in reduced absenteeism, arbitrations, and successful unemployment compensation claims after employee terminations. Usage of sick time in maintenance and production operations dropped from an average of 66.7 hours per employee in 1977 to 36.6 hours in 1983.[14]

A personnel manager at a Goodyear Tire and Rubber Company plant believes that because this approach is less distasteful to the supervisor than the reprimand approach, the supervisor is more apt to administer discipline in a timely and consistent manner than to put off disciplining employees for infractions.[15]

One could ask to what extent this approach eliminates punishment as a means of changing behavior. How do the parties, particularly the subordinates, view the process? Being reminded of or counseled for an offense in the manager's office, perhaps with the manager's boss present, is hardly a cause for rejoicing. Neither is being sent home on a decision-making leave or being told to consider other employment opportunities.

TESTS FOR DETERMINING JUST CAUSE

Over the years, arbitrators have been asked by unions and management to make decisions on thousands of disciplinary cases. One outgrowth of this has been the development of seven principles related to what constitutes fair play with regard to disciplinary action. Because most union-management contracts have agreements that employees can only be disciplined for "just cause," these principles have been labeled as "tests for just cause."[16] The philosophy here is that a firm's disciplinary actions should not be arbitrary, capricious, or unreasonable. Admittedly, most firms in the United States are not unionized. Nonetheless, as we will show in Chapter 2, managers of all firms should be aware of and guided by these principles.

Have Rules/Penalties Been Communicated?

Arbitrators have made it clear that before an employee can be penalized, a firm must communicate the work rules and the penalties for breaking them either through verbal or written communication. Typically this is achieved by means of orientation sessions, employee handbooks, posted lists, or union contracts. Many firms require employees to sign a form stating that they have read the company's rules, understand them, and will abide by them. Managers can also communicate this information through their own words or actions. For example, when managers wear hard hats in construction areas and enforce the rules when employees gamble during their lunch hour, this reinforces the firm's written rules.

One problem sometimes develops when managers do not enforce the written work rules. For example, they may see employees gambling during lunch hour but look the other way even though the prohibition is very clear. This communicates to employees that the written rule is inapplicable and need not be followed. In effect, it does not exist except on paper. Arbitrators have stated that if managers have been inconsistent in rule enforcement, they must first notify employees that henceforth rules will be enforced. They should not take disciplinary action without this forewarning.

There is one important exception to this principle. Certain offenses (e.g., gross insubordination, coming to work intoxicated, selling illegal drugs to coworkers, assaulting others, or theft of company property) are so serious that any employee in our society already knows that such conduct is offensive and heavily punished. Therefore, rules such as these can be enforced even if they have not been communicated.

Is the Rule Necessary?

A second general principle is that a firm's rules should be reasonably related to (1) the orderly, efficient, and safe operation of the business, and (2) the performance that the company might properly expect of the employee. In other words, firms should not have rules based on the personal whims of management. Unless such rules are essential to the success of the organization, they should be eliminated. Take, for example, the case of a truck driver working for a firm that had a specific policy requiring all men to be clean shaven. While on vacation, the driver grew a beard and decided to keep it. Upon returning to work, he was disciplined for it. The arbitrator who heard the case concluded that the rule was not reasonably related to organizational success in this particular instance. The truck driver had minimal public contact, so having a beard appeared to have no adverse effect on the firm's public image. The arbitrator argued, however, that if the employee had a job requiring repeated public contact, his decision might have been different.

One principle that has been established in unionized environments is that even if an employee does not believe a rule is reasonable, he/she must obey it unless there is serious and immediate risk to personal safety and/or integrity. Organizations are not debating societies; hence, orders must be obeyed. Employees should do what they are told and then file a grievance challenging management's right to give the order in the future.

Did the Employee Actually Violate a Rule?

At first glance, it may seem easy to determine whether an employee has broken a company rule or disobeyed an order. One need only compare the employee's behavior with the company's rules or the order. For example, if there is "No Smoking in the Elevator" and the manager sees an employee doing just this, clearly a violation has occurred. Unfortunately, most cases are not so clear-cut. Suppose a manager sees several employees sitting at their desks with their eyes closed. Are they breaking the company's "No Sleeping on the Job" rule? Maybe they are meditating, engaged in deep thought, or praying. In addition, an employee may have fallen asleep because of medication properly prescribed by a physician. If any of these are true, did a rule violation actually occur?

Firms always have an obligation to discover whether the employee did in fact violate or disobey a rule before taking disciplinary action. Employees have a right to know, with reasonable precision, the offense with which they are being charged; and they must be allowed to defend their behavior. Furthermore, arbitrators recommend that an employee's innocence or guilt should not be determined by the individual's past disciplinary record. The only proper use of one's past disciplinary record is in determining the appropriate penalty once the employee has been found guilty of the immediate offense.

Occasionally, a manager may believe that an employee has broken a major work rule but needs time to investigate. In this situation, arbitrators generally recommend that the employee be suspended pending an investigation with the understanding that the final disciplinary decision will be made once the facts have been gathered. Of course, if the investigation fails to support the allegations, the person should be immediately reinstated and given full back pay.

Was the Investigation Conducted Fairly?

Managers have an obligation to investigate a possible rule infraction in a fair and unbiased manner. Arbitrators recommend that even though a manager may be both the prosecutor and the judge, he/she should not also be a witness against the employee. They also recommend that someone other than the manager involved assume the judicial role. This person should be detached from the case and unbiased toward the employee.

Was There Sufficient Proof of Guilt?

Even though analogies to the criminal justice system can be misleading, most arbitrators will consider an employee innocent until proven guilty and the burden of proof rests on the manager. But how much proof does one need? Unfortunately, there is no clear answer. Nevertheless, arbitrator opinions suggest that the evidence must be truly substantial and not flimsy. At least two levels of proof have been put forth. One is "the preponderance of evidence," which is used by civil courts to decide misdemeanor cases. The second is "proof beyond a reasonable doubt." This level is used in deciding felony cases and requires a greater body of evidence. In determining the level of proof needed, some arbitrators suggest that the severity and nature of the offense be considered as well as the expected penalty. There is a difference between charging someone with stealing and charging them with being five minutes late to work. There is also a difference between firing an employee and giving a verbal warning. One recommended guideline is to make the level of proof proportional to the severity of the punishment. Managers may also want to consider whether the disciplinary action will be appealed and what standards are likely to be used by the ultimate "judges" (e.g., other managers, personnel specialists, Equal Employment Opportunity Commission officials, or company lawyers). Keep in mind, however, that disciplinary proceedings are not court cases. In this regard, if a firm dismisses an employee for suspected drug use, the notion of "beyond a reasonable doubt" is less stringently interpreted than it would be if the case were being heard in a court of law.

Was Discipline Administered Evenhandedly?

Arbitrators expect firms to apply rules and penalties evenhandedly and without discrimination. This means that any time employees are caught breaking a rule, they should be subject to disciplinary action. It means that a manager should not ignore misbehavior by one employee while penalizing another. A manager needs to consistently enforce the rules.

Managers also need consistency with regard to the severity of penalties. Employees who have comparable work records and engage in the same misbehavior under similar circumstances should receive the same penalty.

In some cases, company rules may have become outdated and have not been enforced. To be consistent, a manager cannot decide to suddenly enforce the rule. Rather, as noted earlier, one should formally announce that henceforth the rules will be enforced and then do so consistently. If not, eliminate the rule.

Was the Penalty Appropriate?

A final principle of fair play is that penalties need to be reasonably related to (1) the seriousness of the employee's offense, and (2) his/her work record. As we noted earlier, most firms using progressive penalty systems differentiate between serious (major) offenses and less serious (minor) offenses. In addition, they recognize that the breaking of a given work rule can have an array of adverse consequences for the organization. Therefore, penalties need to reflect these differences; the punishment should fit the crime.

Several factors are considered in judging an employee's overall work record. Four major ones appear to predominate:

1. The employee's actual work record—the quantity and quality of one's work. Does the person perform the job well or poorly?
2. The employee's past disciplinary record. Is this the individual's first, second, third, fourth, or more rule infraction?
3. The employee's length of service. How long has the person been working for the firm?
4. Any mitigating or aggravating circumstances. What circumstances surrounded the rule infraction? What caused the employee to break the rule?

Generally speaking, employees who have good work and disciplinary records, have many years of service to the firm, and have overriding mitigating circumstances deserve less of a penalty than those who don't. Keep in mind that the goal in disciplining employees is not to punish them but to get them to change their behavior. A light penalty may be all that is necessary; if so, that's all a manager should give.

Some firms may want to consider factors beyond these listed here. For example, one might want to look at the employee's popularity with other employees when deciding a penalty. Another consideration might be the ease with which the employee can be replaced. A third could be the effects a penalty might have on the offender's mental and physical health. A fourth may be the offender's rank or position in the hierarchy. Any firm is free to use whatever factors it chooses. However, arbitrators typically recommend that firms be consistent in their choice.

CONCLUSION

This chapter has examined a variety of issues related to discipline and punishment. Over the years a controversy has developed about their use. Some have argued that punishment should be avoided because it causes dysfunctional consequences for both the employee and the supervisor. Advocates have countered that punishment is the only feasible and financially justifiable approach a manager can use in some situations. The important question for the manager is not whether punishment should be used but when and how it should be implemented.

The "hot stove" rules make several recommendations about how punishment should be administered. They suggest that action should be taken as soon as possible after an undesirable behavior occurs and that the manager should focus on what the employee did rather than on the employee's personality. Penalties should be administered consistently over time; and prejudice, bias, and favoritism should not enter into the process. In addition, punishment may be more effective if managers provide a clearly understood rationale, tell the employee what can be done to avoid future penalties, and explain the consequences that will follow if the behavior does not improve. Finally, penalties are more effective if they are delivered in the context of a warm and friendly relationship between the superior and subordinate.

If a company is to have a successful disciplinary and penalty system, both the firm and the manager have important roles to play. In practice, companies assume the responsibility of establishing rules, communicating them to employees, and developing a penalty system for enforcing them. By far the most common disciplinary system is the progressive penalty system. An organization can also use the discipline without punishment system, which attempts to minimize the use of punishment and takes a counseling approach. Whichever approach is used, managers would be wise to follow the seven principles of "just cause" that spell out what constitutes fair play with regard to disciplinary action.

The manager's role in the disciplinary process is distinct from that of the organization, yet the two overlap and support each other. Managers have the responsibility for implementing the firm's disciplinary system. This requires that they do several tasks: they must know their organization's rules and be able to compare them with employee behavior to determine if a rule has been broken; they must decide what corrective action needs to be taken and then take it; and they must document whatever action is taken. To the extent that all managers perform these steps effectively, the disciplinary system will be effective and there is a very good chance that employee behavior on the job can be significantly improved.

NOTES

1. D. Caruth, B. Middlebrook, and T. A. Pressley, "This Matter of Discipline," *Supervisory Management*, April 1983, pp. 24–31.

2. R. B. McAfee and W. Poffenberger, *Productivity Strategies: Enhancing Employee Job Performance* (Englewood Cliffs, NJ: Prentice-Hall, 1982).

3. D. Organ and T. Bateman, *Organizational Behavior: An Applied Psychological Approach*, 3d ed. (Plano, TX: Business Publications, 1986).

4. D. McGregor, "Hot Stove Rules of Discipline," in G. Strauss and L. Sayles, eds., *Personnel: The Human Problems of Management* (Englewood Cliffs, NJ: Prentice-Hall, 1967).

5. R. D. Arvey and J. M. Ivancevich, "Punishment in Organizations: A Review, Propositions, and Research Suggestions," *Academy of Management Review* 5, no. 1 (1980), pp. 123–132.

6. A. L. Gary, "Industrial Absenteeism: An Evaluation of Three Methods of Treatment," *Personnel Journal*, May 1971, pp. 352–353.

7. Arvey and Ivancevich, "Punishment in Organizations."

8. Ibid.

9. D. Marholin and D. Gray, "Efforts of Group Response—Cost Procedures on Cash Shortages in a Small Business," *Journal of Applied Behavior Analysis* 9 (1976), pp. 25–30.

10. J. M. Beyer and H. M. Trice, "A Field Study of the Use and Perceived Effects of Discipline in Controlling Work Performance," *Academy of Management Journal* 27, no. 4 (1984), pp. 743–764.

11. R. B. Arvey, G. A. Davis, and S. M. Nelson, "Use of Discipline in an Organization: A Field Study," *Journal of Applied Psychology* 69, no. 3 (1984), pp. 448–460.

12. D. N. Campbell, R. L. Fleming, and R. C. Grote, "Discipline without Punishment—At Last," *Harvard Business Review*, July-August (1985), pp. 48–55.

13. Ibid.

14. Campbell et al., "Discipline without Punishment."

15. J. Huberman, "Discipline without Punishment Lives," *Harvard Business Review* 53 (1975), pp. 6–8.

16. Enterprise Wire Co., 46 LA 359.

Chapter 2

Avoiding Wrongful Discharge, Discrimination, and Defamation Lawsuits

Your administrative assistant has worked for you for fifteen years. Lately, however, her behavior has been changing and she is not carrying her share of the workload as she once did. Her work is often not completed on time; she is very reluctant to learn the new computer program; and she is having trouble getting along with the newer employees. When you've tried to speak with her about these matters, she has brushed you off and has been almost belligerent. Even though the decision will be difficult, you've decided that it's time for a change; you are thinking that you may need to dismiss this employee and find someone new. But can you take action at this point? Over the years you have constantly given her above average to excellent evaluations, and the employee handbook says that the firm may offer employees access to counseling before final action is taken. Moreover, she has not violated any specific rules as stated in the handbook. What actions can you take? What are your responsibilities as an employer? What are her rights as an employee?[1] Can you discipline this employee without setting the firm up for a charge of wrongful discharge or sexual discrimination? What can you tell a prospective employer when she applies for a new job?

Recent laws and a variety of state and federal court decisions since the mid-1960s have radically altered the old employer-employee relationship and in the process have limited a manager's options in terms of taking disciplinary action.[2] Throughout this book we will discuss legal issues in conjunction with particular disciplinary issues. In this chapter we focus on three broad problem areas: wrongful discharge, employment discrimination, and defamation. We also consider what managers and firms can do to reduce potential liability and lessen the possibility for lawsuits.

WRONGFUL DISCHARGE

As we noted in Chapter 1, in unionized firms the contract specifies the terms and conditions of employment and employees can only be disciplined for "just cause." Historically, however, the rules in nonunion situations have been quite different and employers have generally believed that they can discharge at any time for no reason, with or without prior notice. In other words, where no specific time is fixed for the duration of employment and the individual is not provided with a written contract that explicitly states the terms and conditions for continuing employment, the presumption has been that the employment relationship is "at will" and terminable at the pleasure of the employer. In recent years, however, the legislatures and courts in several states have established what amount to exceptions to the at-will employment rule. In other states the concept remains essentially intact although there are a number of restrictions. As Exhibit 2.1 shows, these include limitations on firing when an employee refuses to perform overly dangerous work; firing employees protected by certain state laws because they are gay or overweight; taking retaliatory action against whistle-blowers; and so on. But perhaps the most controversial area of wrongful discharge law is that of implied contracts.

In terms of successful challenges to this aspect of the at-will doctrine, decisions by state supreme courts in New Jersey and Wisconsin (*Woolley v. Hoffman-LaRoche* and *Ferraro v. Koelsch*) have established important precedents.[3] In each case the issue was whether or not an employee handbook could be enforced as a valid and binding contract. Both courts said absolutely yes. For example, the court in *Woolley v. Hoffman-LaRoche* concluded that "the job security provisions contained in a personnel manual widely distributed among a large workforce are supported by consideration and may therefore be enforced as a binding commitment of the employer." In addition, the court said that even an employee who admits that he/she has never read the personnel manual may sue to enforce the "contract." As the law now stands in New Jersey, this is what happens when an employer distributes a personnel manual:[4]

- The employer, by distributing the manual, makes an offer of job terms and conditions.
- By continuing to work after receiving the manual, employees accept the offer.
- The employee's continuing to work also becomes the consideration or "things of value" that must accompany acceptance of the employer's offer in order to create a binding contract.

None of this has to be directly communicated or stated. In the typical case, it all happens automatically whenever the handbook or personnel manual is distributed to any employee.

Exhibit 2.1
Exceptions to the At-Will Doctrine

The At-Will Doctrine states that employers can fire workers for any reason or no reason at all. However, there are numerous exceptions to this, including the following:

1. Civil Rights Act of 1964 prohibits discrimination, including terminating an employee because of race, creed, color, religion, age, sex, or national origin.

2. Employees under contract, such as those in unionized firms, typically have agreements that state they cannot be discharged except for just cause.

3. The Immigration Reform and Control Act of 1986 forbids discrimination, including termination, as a result of citizenship status.

4. The Age Discrimination in Employment Act prohibits discrimination based on age for those over 40 years old.

5. The Employee Retirement Income Security Act (ERISA) precludes discharge for the purpose of denying employees their vested pension rights or denying them the opportunity to vest.

6. The Americans with Disabilities Act of 1992 bans discrimination, including discharge, based on physical or mental disabilities.

7. The Wagner Act or National Labor Relations Act of 1935 makes it an unfair labor practice for an employer to interfere with, restrain, or coerce employees in the exercise of their rights to organize, bargain collectively, and engage in other concerted activities for their mutual aid or protection. This includes encouraging or discouraging membership in any labor organization by discrimination with regard to hiring or tenure or conditions of employment. It also forbids discharging or discriminating against employees because they file charges or give testimony under the Act.

8. The Occupational Safety and Health Act forbids terminating employees for refusing to work when death or serious injury is imminent.

9. Implied contract laws in some states say that when an employee agrees to employment, a contract is created and the employee cannot be fired except for just cause.

10. Various whistleblowing acts protect employees from being terminated for reporting alleged employer violations of statutory policy.

Similarly, the Wisconsin Supreme Court in *Ferraro v. Koelsch*[5] ruled that a handbook in that state will be treated as a binding contract as long as it can be shown that the employee who is seeking enforcement has "accepted" the terms and conditions that the employer "offered." The court in this case found clear proof that the employee had accepted the terms and conditions, because management had required the employee to sign a statement saying, "I have received and read the handbook . . . and

I understand the policies and rules and accept them as a condition of my continued employment."

In each of these cases the primary issue was what constitutes the employment "offer" that provides the basis for a contract. The answer according to the New Jersey and Wisconsin courts is the distribution of a handbook to new employees. That was all the employer (the Hyatt Regency in Milwaukee) did; the court held that by that simple act, management had communicated a contract offer.[6]

Most of the challenges to the at-will rule that have argued the notion of implied contract have relied on the legal theory that "every contract imposes upon each party a duty of good faith and fair dealing in its performance and its enforcement." This implied duty, therefore, effectively says that a manager cannot suspend or terminate an employee unless the reasons are truly honest, consistent with accepted concepts of reasonableness, and in line with the contractual expectations of the parties. For example, discharging long-term employees in order to avoid pension obligations certainly violates good faith and fair dealing.

From a practical point of view, the problem is that if employment is not "at will," then the employer can only dismiss for just cause. In other words, the employee must have engaged in behaviors that are specifically stated as violations of the handbook or personnel manual. If not, the discharge might be considered wrongful. When this happens, most courts can classify the employer's action as tortious and award damages not only for lost wages but also for other "injuries"—such as emotional distress or loss of reputation—that are a direct result of the employer's wrongful conduct. How, then, can a firm protect itself?

Protecting against Wrongful Discharge Litigation

In terms of many of the acknowledged exceptions of the at-will concept, the way to avoid litigation is by knowing the law. Regarding wrongful discharge stemming from an implied contract, legal experts offer a variety of suggestions.

Even though the notion of an implied contract is not universally accepted, the courts in some states clearly do accept it. Therefore, care must be taken not to promise more than the employer is willing to deliver. For instance, close attention should be paid to manuals, handbooks, and other documents suggesting that employment is permanent or that dismissal will only occur for "good cause."[7] It is also generally recommended that firms include an explicit statement that the handbook does not create a contract and that employees can be terminated at will; firms should also inform employees that reasons listed for disciplinary action are not all-inclusive. If the firm is changing an existing handbook, the judicial trend is to require that employees be given adequate notice of such modification. In addition, managers should be careful to avoid specific statements during a job interview that imply a contractual commitment. For example, interviewers would be wise not to suggest that employees are rarely if ever fired or that the applicant can expect a long and prosperous career with the company.

It may also be appropriate for a firm to consider eliminating or at least modifying the use of a probationary period. Many employers require a newly hired employee to serve such a period, and until recently this has been thought to offer greater protection and flexibility for the employer because it provides a trial period during which the employer is free to discharge the individual for little or no reason. The problem is that once the probationary period has ended, an employee may feel that he/she is entitled to job security and will be dismissed only for "good cause." To avoid this possibility, an employer may choose to discontinue the practice of a formal probationary period and, instead, informally observe a new employee's performance and document deficiencies as needed.[8]

Beyond reviewing written documents, it is also generally recommended that a firm evaluate employees' performance on a regularly scheduled basis. These reviews should accurately reflect the individual's performance relative to specific standards and expectations. When a person's performance is so weak that he/she is in danger of being dismissed, any performance review should clearly specify the areas needing improvement, provide a specific time frame within which the employee needs to show improvement, and put the individual on official notice regarding the consequences for noncompliance. Of course, documents should be maintained in readily identifiable and confidential personnel files.[9]

Keep in mind that dismissal is not the only option. For example, if an employee has a long record of good service but has recently been ineffective, it may be that something about the job needs to be changed. Maybe the employee has recently taken on new responsibilities or duties and is now overwhelmed. Redefining the job may put him or her back on track. Problems may also be arising from personality conflicts with peers or from trouble at home. In such cases, an offer of counseling could be the answer.

In situations in which dismissal is clearly necessary, it is usually recommended that the reasons for the employer's action be put in writing. The reasons for the dismissal must be carefully and accurately stated because in subsequent administrative or judicial proceedings, an employer can only rely on the grounds for dismissal originally presented for discharging the employee, even if there were other reasons driving the decision.[10]

Managers also need to examine other personnel practices so as to strengthen employee relations and thereby reduce the need for "at will."[11] For instance, if management could hire the "right" people there would be far fewer "problem" employees. In the orientation of new hires, the firm would be well advised to give clear expectations about what is considered appropriate and inappropriate performance. Subsequent training programs can reinforce the message. Also, managers may require training regarding the handling of problem employees.

Finally, promotions cannot be viewed as a reward for seniority or loyalty rather than effective job performance. When an employee has received regular promotions and is then discharged, questions frequently arise. How could the person warrant the promotions and now be fired? In those unusual cases where such dramatic deterioration of performance actually occurs, it is essential that the situation be well documented.

The rules surrounding discipline and discharge have changed substantially in recent years and are still evolving. There is, however, one rule that doesn't change. If an employer is truly fair in dealing with employees, a wrongful discharge suit is far less likely; and if an action is instituted, the employer is more likely to prevail.[12] In Japan, Great Britain, France, Germany, and Canada, employers are required to show just cause for dismissal. Given this and all the exceptions already noted, it may well be that the attempt to retain at-will employment is not worth the effort.[13]

One last point. Suppose an employee argues that he/she was wrongfully discharged because in order to obtain sufficient proof of guilt the company invaded his/her privacy. Is this a problem? There are, in fact, limitations on certain types of electronic surveillance including the monitoring of telephone conversations unless employees have been duly informed and have given their consent. For example, a firm cannot install covert cameras in restrooms or monitor people as they change their clothes. In addition, personal body searches may lead to problems including charges of assault. But within reason, searching desks and lockers or requesting that employees submit to drug tests or take a polygraph during an ongoing investigation are not a problem. If an employee refuses to comply, wrongful discharge will not come into play unless the actions of the employer are judged to be totally unreasonable.

FEDERAL CIVIL RIGHTS LEGISLATION AFFECTING DISCIPLINE

A second major arena for litigation involves employees who feel that the disciplinary action is discriminatory and a violation of civil rights. In this section we provide a brief overview of federal civil rights laws that are directly related to disciplinary issues. These laws do not prohibit a firm from taking disciplinary action against members of protected groups. However, they do not allow firms to discipline employees because of their race, sex, creed, color, national origin, age, or handicapped status.

Title VII of the Civil Rights Act of 1964

Title VII of the Civil Rights Act of 1964 is without question the centerpiece of federal antidiscrimination law. It prohibits discrimination in terms of any condition of employment on the basis of race, sex, creed, color, or national origin. It applies to most employers (those having fifteen or more employees), labor organizations, and employment agencies.

Title VII was extensively amended in 1972. The Equal Employment Opportunity Commission (EEOC), the agency charged with enforcing the statute, was authorized to file judicial actions. Time limitations were lengthened, coverage was extended to include public employers, and a number of clarifications were added, particularly in the area of religious discrimination. The act was further amended in 1978 to add protection for pregnancy and childbirth.[14]

Reacting to federal court decisions of the 1988–1989 term, Congress passed extensive amendments in the Civil Rights Act of 1991. These amendments, among other things, redefine burdens of proof in disparate impact cases, prohibit discriminatory adjustment of test scores, allow jury trials, and allow damages for intentional discrimination.[15]

The Age Discrimination in Employment Act

Discrimination against persons age forty or over is prohibited by the Age Discrimination in Employment Act (ADEA) of 1967.[16] Although it is similar in wording to Title VII, the ADEA has some defenses and provisions uniquely applicable to age discrimination. Coverage is similar to Title VII, but the ADEA has a distinct enforcement mechanism and, unlike Title VII, allows for the recovery of liquidated damages.

The ADEA draws its operative language from Title VII and thus was intended to receive similar treatment in federal courts. The administrative responsibility originally invested in the Secretary of Labor was transferred by a 1978 amendment to the EEOC.

A 1974 amendment extended coverage to government employees, and further amendments in 1978 expressly prohibited mandatory retirement. Amendments in 1986 eliminated the upper age limit on protection.

The Americans with Disabilities Act (1990) and the Rehabilitation Act (1973)

Discrimination against individuals with physical or mental disabilities is prohibited by two statutes.[17] Coverage of the Rehabilitation Act is limited to government employers, recipients of federal financial assistance, and federal contractors. The Americans with Disabilities Act (ADA) provides protection similar to the 1973 legislation but covers all organizations subject to Title VII.

The ADA is an independent statute, not an amendment to the Rehabilitation Act. Title I, which addresses employment, prohibits discrimination against persons with disabilities by employers subject to Title VII of the Civil Rights Act. The ADA uses more extensive language in defining the scope of protection and the extent of required accommodation of disabilities than does the Rehabilitation Act.

Implications of Civil Rights Laws

The effect of the various civil rights laws, although not specifically directed toward disciplinary actions, is nonetheless important. Clearly, they place an employer on notice that any and all disciplinary decisions must be based on an objective analysis of the employees' behavior and that a supervisor cannot be motivated by bias or prejudice. For example, if an employee is dismissed, there should be well-documented evidence of unacceptable performance or behavior. When the individual in question is a member of any of the groups protected by federal law, this is especially important.

Beyond the legal constraints, good sense would indicate that the more supervisors and managers can operate on the basis of objective facts, the better off everyone will be. The firm will greatly reduce the risk of charges of discrimination and wrongful discharge lawsuits. It will also minimize the risk of companion legal actions under the tort recognized in most states that an individual can sue to recover damages for "intentional infliction of emotional distress." Often the dollar amounts involved here are far larger than for judgments or settlements in discrimination or wrongful discharge actions.

In a case that illustrates this last point, a federal district court in Virginia ruling in *Holland v. First Virginia Banks* awarded punitive damages of $500,000.[18] The plaintiff, a black male, was subjected to intolerable racial name-calling by his supervisor over a period of several months. When he was unable to get the supervisor to stop, he complained to a senior vice president and the problem seemed to be solved. Soon thereafter, Holland was injured on the job, and his supervisor called him at home and told him that he had accepted his resignation. In effect the employee was fired. Holland denied resigning and wrote to ask for his job back. Ultimately, a lawsuit based on racial discrimination was filed. Clearly, firms have much at risk from this type of unwarranted action on the part of managers.

Before dismissing an employee, a firm should look for warning signs of potential problem areas. For example, consider whether the employee is a member of a "protected class" and whether he/she has been treated consistently with all other employees. Also look at past problems with the employee and whether these have been adequately documented. Has the employee been given prior notice of any correctable problems, and was progressive discipline used where appropriate? Finally, be sure that "the punishment fits the crime" and that any mitigating circumstances have been carefully and fully examined.

DEFAMATION

A third broad legal problem comes into play when employees are disciplined, demoted, or discharged, and managers must decide whether other persons inside or outside of the company should be told why. Can an employer legitimately explain such circumstances? What, if any, are the limits and risks of such disclosure? These are questions that, if not properly answered, can lead to claims of defamation.[19]

Consider the following situation. An employee is accused of sexual harassment. The accused individual is interviewed during the course of an investigation of the charge and denies all allegations. Fellow employees who were nearby during the alleged incidents are unable to confirm or deny the events. Following several management meetings to discuss the employer's response, the person is dismissed.

The company then issues a statement regarding the incident. The bulletin mentions the alleged harassment and states that the incident involved "deliberate, repeated, and unsolicited physical contact as well as significant verbal abuse." The bulletin is distributed to all supervisors, who are instructed to cover the key points with their employees. The notice is also read to several hundred employees, verbatim to some and summarized for others. The bulletin is not posted or distributed to employees or parties outside the company. Nevertheless, the discharged employee sues for defamation and malicious slander.

Given these circumstances, is the employer liable for defamation because it issued the formal statement? Can the employer defend its actions by claiming that it was protected by a conditional or qualified privilege to disseminate information about the circumstances surrounding the discharge to both supervisors and the individual's coworkers? These and related questions were addressed in *Garziano v. E. J. DuPont de Nemours and Co.*, in which the example facts were the actual background.[20]

At the trial court level, DuPont claimed a qualified privilege to distribute the written statement to supervisors and advise employees of the circumstances. However, the jury disagreed and awarded the plaintiff $93,000 in compensatory damages.

On appeal, the Fifth Circuit Court, basing its decision on defamation law, concluded that the company had a qualified privilege to disseminate the sexual harassment bulletin, including information regarding Garziano's discharge, to both its supervisors and other employees. The court concluded that the situation was privileged because coworkers had a legitimate interest in the reasons for which a fellow employee was dismissed. DuPont, they said, issued the bulletin under a qualified privilege because:

1. the firm believed that it had a duty to do so,

2. the bulletin was designed to inform employees about the company's position on sexual harassment, and

3. employers are protected in communicating on matters of common interest to employees.[21]

Although the Fifth Circuit ruled in favor of the company, it did remand the case to a jury to determine whether supervisors had unnecessarily distributed the bulletins to third-party independent contractors employed at DuPont facilities. In addition, there were factual issues concerning whether any supervisors elaborated further than the information contained in the bulletin, and how Garziano himself obtained a copy.

As a general rule, courts have accepted the notion of qualified privilege as long as the firm has a legitimate proprietary interest and is attempting to protect itself from similar actions by other employees. For example, in the case of *Schneider v. Pay'N Save Corp.*, the Alaska Supreme Court affirmed the lower court's finding that the employer had a qualified privilege to make statements regarding its belief that an employee, a cashier, had stolen money. The court concluded that the firm was fully justified in attempting to protect against offenses as serious as theft or mishandling of money.[22]

Likewise, in *Deaile v. General Telephone Co.* an employer was permitted to publish to employees the reason for dismissing another employee. The rationale offered for publication was the employer's economic interest in clarifying its policies and preventing future abuse. Another example occurred in *Williams v. Taylor*, in which communications relating to dishonesty of a former employee were made by a manager of a body shop to insurance adjusters who referred business to the shop. In making these communications, the manager was protecting his own interest as well as those of the insurance adjusters.[23]

Courts have even gone so far as to affirm an employer's conditional right to inform others regarding an employee's discharge through communications made in an employee newsletter. In *Zinda v. Louisiana Pacific Corp.*, for example, the Wisconsin Supreme Court held that using the company newsletter to tell others about the reasons for an individual's discharge was legitimate. The court indicated that this communication was reasonable given the fact that termination was for a falsified employment application and that the notice would discourage others from engaging in such conduct.[24]

Even though the courts have given employers considerable freedom in terms of disseminating information, the concept of conditional or qualified privilege is not totally open-ended. An employee may successfully sue for defamation if it can be argued that the firm excessively published the information by telling people who had no real need to know. In addition, all statements must be factual and not motivated by malice. In either case, qualified privilege would not apply. What, then, can a firm do to help protect against such charges? As a first step, before releasing any information the employer should have the employee sign a release that authorizes disclosure and affirms that the facts on file are accurate. Second, the firm should investigate to make sure that the discharge decision was not precipitated by a petty employee/supervisor dispute. When a background of ill will, pettiness, or hostility precedes an employee's dismissal, those are times to limit publication. Third, employers should consider conducting an exit interview so that the employee will fully understand the reasons for the termination. Fourth, make sure that communications are work-related and are disclosed only to those who have a legitimate interest in knowing what happened. Finally, stick to the facts and remember that truth is the ultimate defense. The person's behavior should never be portrayed as being worse than the facts show.[25]

The case of *Lewis v. Equitable Life Assurance Society* shows what can happen when the truth is stretched.[26] This lawsuit involved four employees who were dismissed for what was termed by the company as "gross insubordination." The Minnesota Supreme Court ruled that this was a major overstatement. The employees were actually fired because they refused to lower dollar amounts listed on their expense vouchers that they believed to be valid expenses. Thus, by knowingly overstating what the employees did, the employer became liable for defamation.

This case is also important in that the court ruled that an employer can be liable even if the firm does not directly communicate the information to a third party. The employees themselves disclosed to prospective employers that they were terminated for "gross insubordination." The court held that this self-publication was sufficient communication of a defamatory statement for the former employer to be liable. Clearly, employers must be extremely careful to be completely factual when documenting the reasons for disciplinary actions such as dismissal.

CONCLUSION

There are three broad areas of litigation that directly affect the disciplinary practices and programs of virtually every organization. Across the country wrongful discharge has become an increasingly popular cause for legal action. Even when an employer has gone out of its way to avoid any appearance of a contractual relationship, firms are finding that when they fire without just cause there can be considerable liability. In addition, the list of statutes governing civil rights continues to grow, the most recent addition being the Americans with Disabilities Act enacted in 1990. The simple rule in terms of operating within the bounds of all EEOC legislation is to make sure that all employees are treated fairly and that disciplinary practices are not being used to illegally remove members of protected groups from the organization. Finally, more and more employees are claiming that they have suffered defamation and subsequent loss of reputation as a result of statements made by an employer following disciplinary action. Clearly, employers must be careful here.

As our society becomes ever more litigious, companies can expect an increase in all types of legal actions. It is reasonable to think that situations such as those discussed in this chapter will become more common. Even though it is unrealistic to think that such lawsuits could ever be entirely eliminated, we argue that managers can help to increase the firm's risk by understanding the law and following sound practices when taking disciplinary action. Any organization that wants to protect itself must have flexible, reasonable rules that are understood by all and then must train managers to administer them fairly and exercise good judgment.

NOTES

1. A. Kaplan, "How to Fire without Fear," *Personnel Administrator*, September 1989, pp. 74–76.

2. Ibid.

3. *Ideas and Trends in Personnel* (Commerce Clearing House), no. 92 (May 31, 1985), pp. 81–84.

4. Ibid.

5. *Ideas and Trends in Personnel* (Commerce Clearing House), no. 92 (July 26, 1985), pp. 113–116.

6. Ibid.

7. Kaplan, "How to Fire without Fear."

8. Ibid.

9. Ibid.

10. Ibid.

11. W. Fulmer and A. Casey, "Employment at Will: Options for Managers," *Academy of Management Executive* 4, no. 2 (1990).

12. Kaplan, "How to Fire without Fear."

13. Fulmer and Casey, "Employment at Will: Options for Managers."

14. M. Players, *Federal Law of Employment Discrimination* (St. Paul, MN: West Publishing Co., 1991).

15. Ibid.

16. Ibid.

17. Ibid.

18. Kruchko and Fries, Counselors at Law, *Employee Relations Newsletter.*

19. M. Denis and J. Andes, "Defamation—Do You Tell Employees Why a Coworker Was Discharged?" *Employee Relations* 16, no. 4 (Spring 1991). See also Commerce Clearing House, *Privacy, Defamation and Reference Checks*, 1989.

20. Denis and Andes, "Defamation—Do You Tell Employees Why a Coworker Was Discharged?"

21. Ibid.

22. Ibid.

23. Ibid.

24. Ibid.

25. Ibid.

26. Commerce Clearing House, *Privacy, Defamation and Reference Checks.*

Chapter 3

Using a Progressive Penalty System

Susan works as a sales representative in the Classified Advertising Department of a major newspaper, the *Daily News*. Most of her time is spent talking to individuals who want to place an advertisement in the newspaper's classified section. The level of calls to the department varies from day to day and hour to hour. Sometimes employees are swamped with calls, and at other times they are idle. When the workload is light, employees are asked to call customers back and ask if they want to renew their advertisement. Employees are also asked to do some cold calling (i.e., calling people who place advertisements in other newspapers to see if they want to place an ad in the *Daily News*).

Unfortunately, Susan appears to be inconsistent in terms of calling customers during slow periods. Occasionally she will solicit new business, but usually she finds an excuse or reason for not doing so. The manager has told her on three occasions that soliciting business is important and absolutely required. In response, Susan has made calls for a few weeks and then stopped, or only made a few. She has not made any calls during the last few days even though business has been slow.

As Susan's manager, what would you do? Some type of penalty seems to be in order, but should she be given a verbal warning or a written warning? Is a suspension or even a discharge in order at this point?

As this case demonstrates, managers often have little choice but to take some form of disciplinary action. They may have tried to change the employee's behavior in other ways but have not been successful. In this chapter we examine each step in the progressive disciplinary process. We begin by discussing verbal warnings, then we examine the use of written warnings and suspensions, and then we describe how to conduct termination interviews.

GIVING VERBAL WARNINGS

As we noted in Chapter 1 a verbal warning is typically the first step in a progressive disciplinary system. What should a manager say when conducting the interview? What steps should be followed?

A review of company policies reveals that firms differ in terms of what they call this first step as well as their goals for the process. Some firms call it a verbal warning because emphasis is on warning employees that their behavior is unsatisfactory and that continuing will lead to further disciplinary action, up to and including termination. Other firms call the first step a verbal reprimand and stress telling the employee that the manager is angry and that the employee's behavior must change "or else." This may include "chewing out" the employee. Firms that use the discipline without punishment approach (see Chapter 1) often refer to the first step as a verbal reminder because the goal is to remind the employee of the rule. This assumes that the employee did not know or had forgotten the rule and that a reminder will be sufficient. Yet another alternative is to call the first step a formal counseling session or verbal counseling. This distinguishes it from an informal conversation in which the manager casually asks the employee to change his/her behavior. The emphasis during the formal counseling session is typically on problem solving. The employee's misbehavior is viewed as the problem to be solved, and the goal is to change that behavior. This may involve a determination of why the employee behaved inappropriately. Our point is that there is no one best way for conducting the first disciplinary step. The best approach depends on the goals the manager wants to achieve; of course, one is free to combine the different approaches. Nevertheless, a manager must make sure that employees know they are being officially warned. If the process is too informal, problems can develop.

A case in point involved an employee who returned late to work from a coffee break. Upon seeing the employee, the manager said, "Get on the ball and do your job." Later, the employee stretched his coffee break again and the manager issued a written warning because it was the second offense. The employee immediately filed a grievance, stating that he had never received a verbal warning as required under the union contract and, therefore, the manager was not justified in giving a written warning. The question put before the arbitrator was whether the statement, "Get on the ball and do your job" constituted a verbal warning. What do you think?

In making his decision, the arbitrator noted that the major issue was the firm's past practices with regard to verbal warnings. What is the customary way in which verbal warnings have been given in the past? What have employees learned to expect? The arbitrator ultimately concluded that the manager's actions were not in keeping with past practices, so the employee's grievance was upheld. However, the important conclusion to be drawn from this case is that managers can use any approach they want for the first step as long as it has been explained to employees and they know what to expect.

General Considerations (Principles)

When using the "verbal warning"—or whatever one wants to call the first step—in a disciplinary process, there are several guidelines to follow. First, before taking disciplinary action a manager needs to have just cause (see Chapter 1). This means that the work rules have been communicated to employees, that the rules are essential for organizational success, that the employee actually violated a rule (there was sufficient proof and a fair investigation), that discipline has been administered consistently and even-handedly, and that the penalty was warranted based on the severity of the offense and the employee's work record.

Second, the advice found in the "hot stove" rules (see Chapter 1) is important. The verbal warning should take place soon after the undesired behavior has occurred; penalize the employee's behavior, not his/her personality; penalize consistently; provide a rationale for why the penalty was given and what can be done to avoid future penalties; take disciplinary action within the context of a warm and friendly relationship.

Third, one author has suggested that managers need to avoid the "seven deadly sins" when taking disciplinary action.[1] These are as follows:

1. Failing to obtain all the relevant facts and disciplining based on only hearsay evidence.
2. Disciplining the employee when one is emotionally out of control. This entails losing one's temper and "flying off the handle."
3. Failing to let the employee know the precise reason he or she is being disciplined.
4. Failing to get the employee's side of the story and not letting him or her talk.
5. Letting the employee talk you out of the punishment that should rightfully be invoked.
6. Failing to document what transpired during the disciplinary interview.
7. Holding a grudge against the employee after the disciplinary interview and reminding him/her either verbally or nonverbally about it.

Conducting a Verbal Warning

Even though there are a number of ways of conducting the first step in the disciplinary process, we will focus on two different methods: the verbal reprimand and the verbal counseling session. Both are widely used and have proved successful in various organizations.

The goal of the verbal reprimand approach is to apply the fine art of chewing out an employee in order to effect a behavioral change. This approach has been discussed by Blanchard and Johnson, who call it a "One-Minute Reprimand."[2] The interview may take more than one minute, but the idea is to keep it short. The approach suggests that managers need to begin by forewarning all employees that if they do something wrong, they will be told—and in no uncertain terms. This puts people on notice regarding how they will be treated; so when feedback is negative, it will come as no surprise. When employees do behave inappropriately, Blanchard and Johnson recommend that they be reprimanded immediately—as soon as is practical after the behavior has occurred.

In communicating the reprimand, these authors suggest that the manager tell the employee specifically what is wrong in no uncertain terms. Then, they recommend that the manager state how he/she feels about the employee's misbehavior. This should be followed by a moment of uncomfortable silence so the employee can experience how the manager feels. It also provides the employee with an opportunity to speak up and ask questions. The final step is to remind employees of their value to the firm but that they have erred in this instance. This can be done verbally, or nonverbally by touching the employee on the arm or shoulder or by shaking hands. The final step is for the manager to remember that when the reprimand is over, it is over. Don't hold the incident over the employee's head and keep bringing it up. It is time to get back to business as usual, only now the employee's behavior should have changed.

Consider how this approach might be applied. Assume that John did not get a report to his manager on time; as a result, the boss's own report will be late. What would you say according to the reprimand approach? When John brings in the report late, the following discussion might take place:

The Manager: "John, this report is three hours late. As a result, my report to the boss will also be late and I'm sure I will hear about it. I am very angry about this. (pause for a moment of uncomfortable silence)

John: "I'm sorry, but an emergency came up and I had to solve it."

The Manager: "John, you are a valued employee and overall you are doing an excellent job. However, you must get these reports to me on time."

John: "I will."

The Manager: "Thanks, John. I know I can count on you."

Variations of this approach can be seen by watching sporting events, particularly basketball. A player who is not getting back on defense quickly enough is often called to the bench by the coach. The coach may glare and even yell at the player. Then the coach takes his hand and puts it on the player's shoulder and gently pushes the player back out onto the court. This communicates nonverbally that the coach is generally happy with the player's performance so far, but that the individual's defensive intensity needs to be improved.

Conducting a Counseling Session

The purpose of a "counseling session" or "verbal discussion" or "documented verbal notice" is to change the employee's behavior primarily through problem solving, not through reprimands. The philosophy is that the employee misbehaved for some reason and will continue to do so if the underlying problem is not resolved. For example, employees may be late to work because they were misinformed regarding the correct starting time, or because of traffic problems, a car malfunctioning, baby-sitting difficulties, or any number of other reasons. By determining the true cause of the problem, a manager can develop a workable solution.

One large convenience store chain suggests that managers use the following steps:

1. State the problem by comparing the desired performance with the employee's actual performance.
2. Refer to prior discussions or conversations about the problem.
3. Obtain the employee's response and listen to his or her explanation.
4. Develop a mutually agreeable, specific plan of action that will insure that the problem is corrected. The plan may need to be in writing and include follow-up or review dates and time frames for various actions. Do not accept the statement "I will try harder" as a solution.
5. Tell the employee of possible consequences, including involuntary separation, if performance deficiencies continue.
6. Indicate confidence in the employee's ability to perform correctly.
7. Immediately after the meeting, write an account of the discussion and the agreement reached. Keep this documentation in your own files for future reference.

Let's take an example and see how this approach might be applied:

Mary (Manager): "Tim, I see that you are late to work again. We start at 8:00 and it is now 8:15. This happened last week also, and you will recall that we talked about it."

Tim: "I know I'm late, but my car just hasn't been running right during the last month. First it's one thing, then another. My mechanic thought it was fixed, but obviously it wasn't."

Mary: "We need to come up with a solution to this problem so you won't be late in the future. What suggestions do you have?"

Tim: "Well, I think the car is fixed now. At least that's what my mechanic says."

Mary: "Perhaps a backup plan would be helpful so that in case your car doesn't work, you can still be here on time."

Tim: "Well, I'll check with one of my neighbors and see if they can bring me to work in an emergency."

Mary: "That sounds fine. Just remember that it's critical that you be here on time and that if you aren't, you are subject to further disciplinary action up to and including involuntary discharge."

Tim: "I understand that and won't be late again."

Mary: "You have been an excellent employee since joining us a year ago, and I am confident you can get this tardiness problem solved."

Notice that the emphasis here is on developing a solution to Tim's tardiness problem. In this regard, three options are available. The manager can develop the solution and tell the employee what it is. However, the problem with this approach is that if the solution doesn't work, the employee can blame the manager. In addition, if the employee is so inclined, he/she can make sure the manager's solution fails. In either case the manager loses. Alternatively, the manager can suggest possible solutions and let the employee choose one of them. This approach may be effective, but it is possible that the manager's alternatives may not include the best solution. Therefore, the better approach is usually to let the employee develop the ultimate solution. Workers are more likely to keep commitments if they feel a sense of ownership. Sometimes, during the interview an employee will indicate that he/she cannot think of a solution. In this case the manager may want to suggest that the employee think about the issue and continue the discussion later.

Documenting the Disciplinary Action

Regardless of which approach one chooses in conducting the first step in the disciplinary process, it is very important that managers have a written account of the discussion and place this information in their own files. The manager needs to describe the incident and the discussion in the event that the employee is ultimately terminated and initiates a wrongful discharge suit or grievance. Even though someone may have an excellent memory, the details of a specific case can easily be forgotten, and few courts or arbitrators are likely to rule in the firm's favor. This explains why the first step is often referred to as a documented verbal warning. Exhibits 3.1 and 3.2 show two different documentation forms, and Exhibit

Exhibit 3.1
Verbal Warning Documentation Form

Employee (print)_____Store_____

Supervisor (print)_____Date_____

A. Describe in detail examples of the employee's unsatisfactory performance.

B. When was this discussed with the employee?

C. What was the employee's response to your verbal warning?

D. Describe the agreements reached between you and the employee to solve the behavior problem.   What time period was set?   What follow-up date was given?

Supervisor's Signature_____

Exhibit 3.2
Verbal Counseling Session Documentation Form

Employee Name:_____ Position:_____

Date:_____ SSN: _____

1. Area of Concern:

2. Goal/Objective to be achieved:

3. Steps to achieve goal:

4. Other comments:

Follow up Date_____ to review progress and results.

Employee Signature: _____ Date:_____

Manager's Signature: _____ Date:_____

3.3 shows a letter. The specifics of what should be included in the documentation will be described toward the end of this chapter.

CONDUCTING WRITTEN WARNINGS

The written warning is typically the second step in the progressive penalty process. It is viewed as a more severe form of discipline than a verbal warning because the warning form becomes a part of the employee's personnel file. Although its main purpose is to change the offender's behavior, it may have the added advantage of deterring others. When the word spreads around, other employees learn that a given behavior is unacceptable. This reduces the probability of others becoming offenders.

Three situations give rise to a written warning. One is when an employee breaks a "minor" work rule for a second time. A second takes place when a minor work rule is broken but the infraction is sufficiently severe that a written warning is deemed necessary on the first offense. The last occurs when an employee's quantity and quality of work fall below acceptable standards and previous discussions have not corrected the problem.

The guidelines for giving written warnings are identical to those for conducting verbal warnings, that is, follow the "hot stove" rules, be sure you have just cause, and avoid the "seven deadly sins." However, there is a difference between the two in terms of the content of the disciplinary interview.

Preparing for the Written Warning Interview

Numerous guidelines have been suggested to prepare for the written warning interview. Perhaps the most common is to select a quiet, private location. The discussion may take place in the manager's office or at a neutral site. Another recommendation is for the manager to organize and

Exhibit 3.3
Documented Verbal Warning Memo to Employee File

April 26, 199X

    I had a discussion today with Harvey Southworth concerning three instances of tardiness in the past two weeks. I told him that he had been more than 10 minutes late to work on April 15, 12 minutes late on April 18, and 9 minutes late today. He agreed he had been late those days. I reminded him of the importance of being to work on time and told him that continued tardiness would not be tolerated.

have available all relevant information obtained from the investigation, including documents, records, and testimony.

Many firms suggest that managers complete the written warning form prior to conducting the interview. This approach may speed the interview process and eliminate the need to do extensive, and perhaps intimidating, writing during the interview. On the other hand, some organizations prefer that the form be completed during the interview itself so that any new facts uncovered during the interview can be entered. A third approach is for managers to complete the form but leave it in the desk until it is determined whether any new information has been revealed during the interview. If so, the completed form is left in the desk and a new document is prepared during the interview or no written warning is given. If not, the manager takes the completed form out of the desk and discusses it with the employee. Two examples of written warnings are shown in Exhibits 3.4 and 3.5.

What should one include on the form, regardless of when it is completed? The information should be sufficiently complete that a person who is totally unfamiliar with the case could read it and know exactly why the employee is being disciplined and what transpired during the written warning interview. Keep in mind that whatever is written may be scrutinized by courts, lawyers, personnel managers, grievance committee members, union officials, and arbitrators. In essence, the form should present an accurate, play-by-play account of what happened.

Because there is no one definitive list of items to include on the written warning form, some firms use comprehensive forms that allow managers to answer specific questions and fill in all boxes. Exhibit 3.6 provides a listing of typical items. How this might look in a letter is indicated in Exhibit 3.7.

Conducting the Written Warning Interview

Firms use different methods in conducting written warning interviews just as they do in conducting verbal warnings. Some emphasize problem solving, some reprimands, and some the warning aspect. One large convenience store chain trains its managers to use the following approach:

1. Begin the meeting by telling the employee that he/she is being given a written warning.
2. Explain the purpose of the meeting and let the employee read the written warning form.
3. Refer to previous conversations related to the problem (if any), including prior verbal warnings.
4. Listen to the employee's response.

Exhibit 3.4
Written Warning Form

Employee's Name:_____Job Title:_____

Violation:

___Absenteeism
___Tardiness
___Fighting
___Horseplay
___Substance Abuse
___Dress Code
___Other-give rule number_____

Date of Rule Violation:_____

Number of Other Disciplinary Action Notices on File_____

---

1. Detail What Occurred, Where, When, and How:

2. Employee Comments:

3. Action to be Taken if same violation occurs again:

Date this notice was given:_____

Supervisor's Signature:_____

Employee's Signature:_____

Witness (if needed): _____

Exhibit 3.5
Written Warning Form

Employee's Name:_____Number_____

Position:_____Department_____

1. Description of Incident (Spell out step by step what occurred.
Give times, witnesses, rules broken):

2. Manager's Comments:

3. Employee's Comments:

I acknowledge that I have read this form. My signature does not
necessarily mean that I agree with the action taken against me.

Employee Signature   Manager's Signature

Department Manager's Signature   Director of H. R. Signature

This form is to be submitted to the Human Resources Department
within three days after completion.

Exhibit 3.6
Suggested Items to Include on Written Warning Form

1. Who warning is to (employee's full name and social security number or company number).
2. Who warning is from (supervisor or manager).
3. Dates: date of warning conversation, date of rule infraction, and date form was filled out.
4. If written warning is given for a specific performance problem (insufficient quantity or quality of work), describe in detail the employee's behaviors that have created the problem. What has the employee done that is unsatisfactory—give dates and times of occurrences, specific quotes, and any witnesses. Detail what, when, and where.
5. If the written warning is for a rule infraction, state exactly what the employee has done that constitutes a rule infraction. Describe the incident chronologically, giving times, places, witnesses, and what was said. State the rule that the employee has broken.
6. Refer to any previous conversations related to this warning.
7. State the specific changes you expect from the employee and the time frame.
8. Indicate the possible consequences, including involuntary separation, if performance deficiencies or violation of policy continues.
9. Write down any employee comments related to the warning.
10. Sign the written warning form.

---

5. Tell the employee the specific behavior you expect.
6. State that if further rule infractions occur, the employee is subject to further disciplinary action up to and including termination.
7. Develop a plan to correct the problem along with time frames, if necessary.
8. Sign the written warning form (if you have not already done so) and ask the employee to do the same. If the employee refuses, obtain a witness or ask the employee to write on the back of the form that he/she refuses to sign and then ask him to sign that he refused. Alternatively, send a copy of the warning to the employee's home via registered mail and retain the receipt for your files. Give a copy of the form to the employee.
9. Indicate your confidence that the employee's behavior will change.

SUSPENDING EMPLOYEES

Suspension without pay is usually the third step in the progressive penalty system. Suspensions can range in length from one day to six months,

Exhibit 3.7
Written Warning Letter

To: Sandra Davis

From: Maria Consolvo

Re: Performance Problems

April 22, 1991

In recent months your editing has not been up to the standards I expect of an experienced copy editor. There have also been incidents when you failed to carry out specific assignments. As a result of your high rate of editing errors and inefficiencies, the pages you are responsible for require extraordinary double-checking and backup attention. In short, you have not been paying proper attention to your duties and have relied on others to catch errors you should not have permitted to be made in the first place.

Specifically:

1) You have allowed too many typographical errors -- errors of spelling, style, and substance -- to exist in items typed by the clerks. Despite our previous discussions of these errors, there is little evidence you are making positive efforts toward attaining the goal we set -- no more than one typographical error per day on your pages.

2) You have not double-checked copy you have prepared before sending it to the typesetter. Specifically, embarrassing errors have appeared in information boxes you have prepared; last Sunday, a section-front index box had two typos, one of which was a misspelling of "Hampton." There have also been errors and typos in photo captions you have written recently. Copies of these errors, most of which we have discussed, are attached.

3) On March 13, you left work without releasing two pages that had to be completed that day. The art on one page had to be reshot to fit. Your absence was dereliction of duty.

These repeated incidents of poor editing and omissions of duties cannot be tolerated. I expect that you will immediately apply yourself to the task of editing carefully the pages for which you are responsible to ensure they are free of errors of fact, style, spelling, grammar and context. Unless your performance improves demonstrably, you will be subject to disciplinary action up to and including termination.

but the average is approximately three days. The idea is to modify behavior by impressing upon employees the severity of their offense and to make them aware that continued misbehavior is likely to result in termination. By being sent home, the person gets a small taste of what unemployment will be like. The employee may also experience social pressure to change his/her behavior from family, friends, and coworkers.

Keep in mind that suspensions also deter other employees from violating rules. They see that a coworker is absent and recognize that a given behavior is unacceptable. This may reduce the likelihood of them misbehaving.

Some firms substitute a final written warning for a suspension because of the hardship imposed by having an employee absent. This is particularly true for small firms, such as convenience stores and gas stations, where only one or two employees are on duty and short-term replacements are not readily available. Also, some firms question the logic of using suspensions at all. They argue that suspending an employee, particularly for absenteeism, seems contradictory. Because you want the person to come to work every day, why suspend them? To do so insures that they will not be at work.

Various occasions give rise to a suspension. One occurs when an employee breaks a minor work rule for the third time. Another occurs when an employee breaks a major work rule for the first time. A third occurs when an employee's quantity and quality of work fall below acceptable standards and previous discussions of written warnings have not corrected the problem. In sum, an employee is suspended at most firms when—in a manager's judgment—a written warning is insufficient and a termination is too strong a penalty, at least right now. Once again, judgment comes into play.

There is one other unique occasion when suspensions are given. Some firms use it as a holding action or a way to buy time. For example, a manager may need time to determine an employee's innocence or guilt when investigating an offense such as fighting or stealing. By suspending the employee, the manager can conduct an inquiry without the employee being present. When the case has been completed, the manager can either take disciplinary action or reinstate the employee with back pay. Suspensions are also used by many firms that require managers to obtain approval from the Human Resources Department or chief executive officer (CEO) before terminating an employee. Rather than enforcing summary dismissal, these firms tell managers to suspend first, obtain approval, and then call offenders back to the firm and terminate them.

The general guidelines for giving suspensions are identical to those for conducting verbal and written warnings: follow the "hot stove" rules, be sure you have just cause, and avoid the "seven deadly sins." In addition, the guidelines for preparing for and documenting the suspension interview are the same. However, there is a small difference in terms of the contents of the interview itself. When suspending an employee, the manager needs to refer back to the prior written warning conversation (not the verbal warning conversation) and tell the employee that he/she is being suspended (not being given a written warning) without pay, and for how long.

TERMINATING EMPLOYEES

Terminations constitute the last and final step in the typical progressive penalty system. Clearly, the goal is not to rehabilitate employees or attempt to change behavior, but to rid the firm of dangerous or disruptive employees. Employees are usually terminated for three major disciplinary reasons: (1) if they have violated a minor work rule for the fourth time; (2) if they have violated a major work rule—such as fighting, stealing, harassing, and so on—for the first time; (3) if their quantity or quality of work remains unsatisfactory despite previous discussions.

The termination process offers significant risk of litigation based on discrimination or wrongful discharge. Therefore, firms must take various precautions before firing anyone. Generally, managers would be wise to:

1. Be sure that the rule broken was reasonably related to organizational success.
2. Make certain that the rule or the expected quantity or quality of work had been communicated to the employee.
3. Investigate employee misconduct thoroughly and quickly.
4. Ensure that one has sufficient evidence of employee misconduct.
5. Make sure that the termination is consistent with past organizational practice and that there is no discrimination.
6. Check to see that terminating the employee is appropriate given the severity of the offense and the employee's work record.

In sum, many legal experts and arbitrators recommend that employees be discharged only for just cause, even though the at-will doctrine may allow a manager to fire someone for any reason or no reason at all. By following just cause, the chances of a grievance or a wrongful discharge suit should be decreased because employees are likely to feel they have been fairly treated. Those who feel they have been abused are much more likely to retaliate.

Weighing the Discharge Decision

In many cases, the discharge decision is not an easy one. The employee may have been with the firm for some time, and the person undoubtedly has certain compensating strengths or positive attributes. In addition, the firm may have spent a considerable sum of money on training and the employee may be well liked by coworkers, customers, and even management.

Thus, many firms are hesitant to fire and will consider other alternatives first. A common response is to transfer the employee to another department or job. The general rule for doing this is to transfer the employee if he/she has a real chance to succeed on the new job. Do not transfer if it means dumping the problem on someone else. Although this may solve one problem, it is likely to be detrimental in the long run. Keep in mind, however, that an employee's job performance is determined by a combination of ability and motivation. An employee may have the skills needed to perform effectively in a new job, but does he/she want to? Both aspects of this equation need to fall in place before a transfer is appropriate.

Occasionally, a manager may have a personality clash with a subordinate. The manager may get along well with others, as does the subordinate, but for some reason the two simply don't work effectively together. In this case a transfer may also make sense.

Related to transferring is to demote or—in rare cases—to promote the offending employee. Once again, the general rule is to do so only if one is convinced that the employee will succeed in the new job. Sometimes employees have been promoted to jobs that are beyond their capabilities and their performance suffers. In other cases the performance is substandard because the employee dislikes the job. In both situations a demotion may be appropriate. However, a critical issue is whether the employee can accept being demoted. Demotions work best if both the manager and the employee view it as a good idea.

Promoting problem employees is generally not encouraged. Most firms argue that this simply rewards unacceptable behavior and that employees must develop a favorable track record before any promotions are warranted. Why do some firms promote these employees? Some cannot or do not want to terminate the employee. Hence, they move the person into a position in which he/she becomes relatively powerless and harmless. Other firms promote such people because they believe the employee is overqualified for the present job and that this is the reason for the problem. The hope is that the employee will perform the new job well because it is more challenging and interesting. The critical issue is how likely it is that the employee will be effective in the new job.

Some companies may even attempt to get employees to quit so that they do not need to fire them. They may suggest or imply that the employee would be happier elsewhere. If the person does not quit, pressure may be brought through undesirable work schedules or poor job locations. The problem is that the employee may have nowhere else to work. In addition, some employees don't get the hint that they are unwanted. Thus, the plan goes awry and the poor performer remains. The problem with this approach is that courts in many cases have deemed this treatment to be "constructive discharge." In other words, the firm has made life so unbearable that any reasonable person would consider the situation intolerable. In a case in Massachusetts, for example, an employee had been given new duties and demoted. He resigned, filed suit, and won.

Another alternative is to retrain the employee and assign the person the same job. The rationale is that the employee's misbehavior may have resulted from a lack of appropriate knowledge rather than a lack of motivation. Training may teach employees new skills, re-energize them through increased self-confidence, help them see the importance of their job more clearly, and clarify certain misunderstandings. The critical question is this: What are the chances that the person's behavior will improve after retraining? Some firms favor this approach because if the training fails to improve performance, neither the union nor the employee is likely to argue that a termination wasn't warranted.

When the problem appears to be the result of a psychological or medical condition, rehabilitation may be an alternative to immediate dismissal. Perhaps the employee is burned out, is experiencing stress due to job-related or family problems, or is physically or mentally ill. Firms often refer such cases to medical doctors, psychotherapists, and social workers. In fact, larger firms may even require that the worker contact a counselor associated with the organization's Employee Assistance Program (EAP; see Chapter 8). The issue once again is whether sending employees to rehabilitation will lead to greater job performance and if the firm is in a position to offer long-term assistance.

Finally, a firm may attempt to address poor performance by reassigning tasks. If an employee does not do a particular task well, some firms assign it to someone else. The risk here is that employees may come to believe that the way to get rid of any onerous job task is to do it poorly. In so doing, they slowly reduce their duties to only those they enjoy. Another problem is that other employees may resent being asked to take on additional responsibilities. One solution is to require that employees swap duties equally (i.e., one employee trades the task he/she performs poorly for another task deemed appropriate by all concerned). Although this may be possible in some firms, it may not be in some situations, small firms, or unionized firms that adhere rigorously to job descriptions.

Benefits of Discharging Employees

Managers are often hesitant to terminate employees because of their concern for the employee's welfare. They recognize that the employee may suffer emotional scars as well as economic adversities. These are important considerations. Nevertheless, there are times when discharge is the best option. Problem employees are often disliked by coworkers who have to cover for and assist them. When the chronic offender is terminated, the morale of these other employees may actually improve. In addition, there are direct economic costs resulting from work being done badly or not at all. Continuing to employ these people amounts to putting offenders on corporate welfare.

Another benefit of termination is that it sends a clear signal that misbehavior is not acceptable. This not only discourages others from misbehaving but may also motivate them to improve performance. Terminations, then, may improve an entire department's productivity.

Perhaps the major benefit to the manager is that the problem employee is no longer around to create turmoil. Such employees have a way of draining one emotionally. They create sleepless nights and can dominate a manager's mental processes. Firing eliminates this problem.

Timing the Discharge

When to terminate an employee depends upon the reasons for firing the employee. Was a work rule broken, or is the worker's quality and/or quantity of work insufficient? In the former case, a manager has little choice but to terminate shortly after the rule infraction occurs. For example, if an employee is caught stealing, most firms would fire almost immediately. In practice, many firms instruct managers to suspend employees, pending termination, rather than firing them on the spot. The manager then conducts an investigation of the incident to determine whether sufficient proof of guilt exists. If so, the manager seeks formal authorization to terminate, calls the employee back to the job site, and dismisses him/her.

On the other hand, if an employee is being discharged for poor quality or quantity of work, a manager often has more options. Consider two different scenarios. Assume that Person A is a poor or marginal performer most of the time and then, suddenly, does an extremely inaccurate job, causing the firm considerable embarrassment. In this case it makes sense to terminate immediately, following the approach used when a rule is broken.

Now consider Person B, whose work has been deteriorating steadily for the past few months. The person has been repeatedly warned but the situation has still not improved. In this case the manager has considerable leeway. The person could be fired now, any time over the next few weeks, or even several months from now.

As a general rule, firms should avoid firing someone who has just returned from a leave of absence such as for childbirth, military service, jury duty, a temporary disability, or a vacation. Furthermore, a discharge is not advisable immediately after an employee has filed a grievance or lawsuit, before the vesting of pension benefits, or before an important event such as a birthday, wedding anniversary, or important holiday. Firing employees at such times is likely to make them particularly resentful and lead to wrongful discharge action suits. Also, these discharges can result in adverse publicity leading to public backlashes and boycotts. Imagine the case of an employee with many years of loyal service who is suddenly fired the day before Christmas and right before pension vesting, with five minutes' notice. The employee is humiliated and takes the story to the news media, which has a field day with it.

Another suggestion for managers is to avoid firing when angry and not emotionally in control. Under these circumstances the wrong words may be said, providing the employee with a stronger legal case.

Who Should Conduct the Termination Interview?

Traditionally, the termination interview has been conducted by the offender's immediate supervisor. However, one author[3] suggests that an immediate supervisor should not face the employee when:

1. Emotions are running high and an ugly confrontation might develop;
2. The employee is expected to be belligerent and possibly violent;
3. The employee is likely to challenge the termination through lawsuits or the filing of grievances and appeals;
4. The supervisor is new and does not know how to conduct a termination interview;
5. The manager does not handle termination interviews well.

Preparing for the Termination Interview

Preparation for the interview begins with gathering the facts that justify the termination and asking a higher authority to review them and grant permission to discharge. Even if it is not required by company policy, most experts recommend that the manager ask at least one other person to review the case. This person should be high ranking enough to be objective but low enough to be knowledgeable about the circumstances and the situation.[4] It is not unusual to have termination letters or forms that need to be completed during the preparation stage (see Exhibit 3.8). Some firms even prepare a resignation letter in the event that this option is offered to the employee.

At this point the supervisor needs to obtain information regarding the worker's fringe benefits and final paycheck. This involves the employee's life insurance, medical coverage, accrued vacation pay, pension plan, credit union accounts, and other contractual obligations. One large convenience store chain has prepared a checklist of these to insure that the manager is properly prepared.

Exhibit 3.8
Termination Form

Employee Name (First, M.I., Last):_____

Street Address:_____

City/State/ZIP:_____

Home Phone:_____

Social Security Number:_____

TERMINATION DATA:

Last day worked:_____ Check Disposition:_____

Eligible for Rehire: ___YES ___NO
Eligible for Unemployment ___YES ___NO
Termination by: _____

Employee Review:
    Ability   ___ Satisfactory ___ Unsatisfactory
    Attendance   ___ Satisfactory ___ Unsatisfactory
    Work Performance   ___ Satisfactory ___ Unsatisfactory
    Attitude   ___ Satisfactory ___ Unsatisfactory

TERMINATION INTERVIEW:

Manager's Statement:

Employee's Statement:

_____   _____
Employee's Signature   Manager's Signature   Date

Having a witness is often recommended. This person can serve as a bodyguard, can run for help if an emergency arises, and can fetch needed information. More important, the witness can vouch for what was or was not said during the interview. He or she can also act as a calming influence on the participants and can help answer questions and resolve disagreements.

A final task is to select a suitable location for the termination interview. Most firms conduct it in the manager's office. Others feel that a neutral site away from the work area may be more appropriate. The primary considerations are privacy, freedom from distractions, and an atmosphere conducive to rational conversation.

Conducting the Termination Interview

The major goal of the termination interview is to explain why the employee is being fired in such a way that the person will not become so angry as to file a lawsuit or grievance. Thus, firing must be done in a calm and professional manner, with no vindictiveness or malice. This is no time to berate the employee for the last time or to make an example of someone.

The interviewer usually begins by telling the employee that he/she is being discharged as of a specific date. One recommendation is to "be blunt and not brutal." Don't apologize or be tentative in any way, because this could indicate that you might be willing to change your mind. Don't tell the employee that his/her services are not needed or that the firm is going to have to "let him/her go." Instead, tell the employee bluntly that he/she is being terminated. This eliminates any chance that the employee might believe he/she is being laid off or placed on a leave of absence.

The next step is to explain why the discharge is necessary. This involves reviewing the performance problems or rule violations that led up to the termination. It is important to gather all prior records and relevant facts so that questions can be answered quickly. This is also an opportunity for the manager to let the employee vent frustrations. Keep in mind that it is better for the manager to listen than to have the employee go and talk to an attorney. One other recommendation is not to allow the employee to change the outcome. Once the decision has been made, it should be adhered to unless significant new information related to the case suddenly becomes available.

Now that the employee knows why he or she is being terminated, the next step is to explain what will happen to his/her fringe benefits—medical insurance, life insurance, vacation accrual, and so on. The manager should have obtained this information during the preparation stage, so now it just needs to be explained.

Some firms recommend that employees be asked to sign a termination letter (Exhibit 3.9) or form (Exhibit 3.8). Others suggest that the employee be allowed to resign and be provided with a resignation form instead. The argument in favor of resignation is that the employee may be less inclined to file a lawsuit. However, forced resignations may be considered by courts as "constructive discharge," in which case the company can still be liable for wrongful discharge. However, this doesn't change the fact that a resignation may reduce the likelihood of legal action.

At this point the interview is over unless the employee has further questions. The best advice is to listen to the questions, answer them, and try not to be argumentative. One question that occasionally arises is whether the firm will serve as a reference for the employee. Many organizations have specific policies covering the release of information regarding prior employees to prospective employers. Another issue is whether the employee is entitled to severance pay. The firm may consider offering this in return for having the employee sign a waiver releasing the firm from further liability. To be enforceable, this document must be signed voluntarily and without duress.

The Aftermath

Once the interview is over, many managers believe their job is finished. However, in many ways it has just begun. The manager still needs to retrieve company property possessed by the employee, make sure the individual leaves the premises, document the interview, and inform others who have a legitimate need to know.

Employees often have on their person or in their work area property that belongs to the firm, and this must be collected. Some firms keep lists of equipment issued to employees, so a check of this list can insure that all property is returned.

Several approaches can be used to make sure the employee leaves the premises. One is for the manager to take the employee back to the work area, assist in picking up all personal belongings, and then escort him/her off company property. This approach is good if no or few employees remain in the work area. But if the area is busy, the terminated employee could be unduly embarrassed. An alternative is to usher the person off the site now but allow the person to pick up personal belongings at a later time. A third approach is to escort the employee off the premises now and send personal possessions in the mail. The risk here is that the employee may contend that something was stolen. In addition, the manager may not know which property belongs to the firm and which to the employee. The one situation to avoid is letting the employee return to the work area unescorted. Employees have been known to steal or destroy company property on the way out the door. Keep in mind that once someone has been fired, they may see little to lose by being destructive.

Exhibit 3.9
Termination Letter

To: Joe Smithers' personnel file

From: Mary Jones

Re: Termination of Joe Smithers

April 19, 1991

     This memo is to document the conversations I had today with
Joe Smithers concerning his driving a company vehicle with a
suspended driver's license.

     Human Resources informed me this morning that Joe's license
has been suspended for two weeks. I confirmed with the Payroll
office and his Zone Supervisor that he had worked and driven a
company vehicle during the suspension. I left a message for Joe to
see me as soon as he got into the office.

     When Joe came in, I told him that his driving record indicated
he had driven a company vehicle without a valid driver's license.
He explained that he did not know about the suspension because DMV
had not mailed him anything about it. He confirmed that he had not
paid the fine for a speeding ticket but added that DMV had not told
him his license would be suspended for not paying. He acknowledged
that he had signed the Driver Orientation Checklist, had heard a
discussion of the company's suspended-license policy in the
defensive driving class, and had not informed his supervisor that
his license was suspended. I reminded Joe of the policy that an
employee will be terminated for driving a company vehicle without
a valid driver's license. I gave him the opportunity to check with
DMV to see if there was a mistake in his records.

     Joe called me back this afternoon with additional information,
but it did not contradict the motor vehicle record showing that his
license had been suspended for not paying a fine. (Joe said DMV
sent notices to his old address; he moved two months ago but did
not tell DMV.) After conferring with the Circulation and Human
Resources directors, I then informed him that he was terminated.

c: Circulation Director, Human Resources Director

Documenting the termination involves the same process discussed earlier for suspensions and written warnings. The goal is to state the facts
that precipitated the termination and what was said during the interview
in such a way that someone totally unfamiliar with the case would know
what happened. Exhibit 3.9 gives an example of an effective letter.

   Once the employee has left and the documentation is complete, the
manager must now inform others. Members of the Personnel Department
need to be told, as do other managers including, perhaps, the CEO. It is
also wise to tell those in charge of security not to let the discharged employee back on company property. The issue of what to tell employees is

the more difficult one. As we discussed in Chapter 2, charges of malicious slander and defamation of character are a possibility if the wrong things are said. When customers or people outside of the firm ask for Ralph, the best response might be, "Ralph is no longer employed here. Mary has taken his place. May she help you?"

CONCLUSION

This chapter has closely examined the major steps in the progressive penalty system. This information is important because virtually every manager periodically needs to take disciplinary action. Furthermore, managers often dread this task because of a lack of confidence. They fear that the employee will become angry or that his/her behavior will not improve. Given that many firms do not train managers in this area, these feelings are understandable. The information presented in this chapter should be helpful in reducing this fear and increasing the likelihood of success.

The progressive penalty system entails four steps: a verbal warning, a written warning, a suspension, and a discharge. However, these steps are not etched in stone; firms may add or delete steps as they wish. Each organization has unique characteristics, so the challenge is to develop a system that fits with them. Unfortunately, many organizations use the four-step process because others use it, thereby failing to maximize the potential of a custom-made system.

One of the most important concepts to remember is that a firm's progressive penalty system cannot be viewed in isolation. Rather, it is part of a firm's overall motivation and leadership system. If a manager frequently needs to discipline employees, there may be shortcomings elsewhere. Perhaps the jobs are boring and lack challenge. The pay and fringe benefits might be unsatisfactory. Supervision might be punitive or incompetent. Managers may need to address these issues and cannot expect the disciplinary system to be the only force for enhancing or maintaining high performance.

NOTES

1. L. L. Steinmetz, *Managing the Marginal and Unsatisfactory Performer*, 2d ed. (Reading, MA: Addison-Wesley Publishing, 1985).

2. K. Blanchard and S. Johnson, *The One-Minute Manager* (New York: Berkley Books, 1982).

3. L. V. Imundo, *Employee Discipline: How to Do It Right* (Belmont, CA: Wadsworth Publishing, 1985).

4. L. L. Steinmetz, *Managing the Marginal and Unsatisfactory Performer.*

Chapter 4

Dealing with Employee Insubordination

Sam was the manager of a retail establishment that had six employees. Because Sam owned only a small portion of the company, he was actually responsible to two other men who jointly owned the controlling interest in the business.

Karol had worked for the firm for twenty years, starting with the founder of the firm. Karol liked to talk constantly about literally nothing to other employees and customers from opening until closing, causing Sam to wonder about his usefulness. Karol's talking sometimes made it impossible for him to hear customers. On one occasion he had not heard a customer express a desire to purchase an item, and the customer had walked out without buying while Karol merely continued to talk.

Karol had been taking Saturday afternoons off to attend the local high school's football games. One fall, Karol announced on Tuesday that he would be taking Friday and Saturday off so that he could have a four-day weekend (Thursday was Thanksgiving Day) and attend a family reunion. Sam responded that he would let Karol have Friday or Saturday off but not both, because other employees had also asked for time off and it was impossible to let two employees off at the same time. Karol maintained that he was going to take both days off.

Sam took the problem to one of the owners, who called Karol and asked him to come over to his house to talk about the situation. Karol refused and said there was nothing to talk about—he was going and that was that.

In this example, Karol has refused to comply with two different management requests. His behavior constitutes what many firms consider to be insubordination. We will examine this concept by describing the different employee behaviors that constitute insubordination, present company policies, and identify the actions a manager needs to take or avoid when dealing with insubordination.

WHAT IS INSUBORDINATION?

It has long been recognized that managers have the right to determine those jobs that need to be performed and to ask employees to do them. They have the right to direct the work force, to plan, and to direct and control all business operations. This is essential if the firm is to succeed. By the same token, employees have an obligation to do what is asked of them and to avoid undermining management's authority.

The concept of insubordination ultimately relates to these two employee obligations. More specifically, employees are deemed insubordinate if they fail to obey a direct order or if they undermine the manager's authority by using abusive language, physical assault, or threats. Unfortunately, neither of these issues is clear-cut.

TYPICAL INSUBORDINATION POLICIES

Company policies covering insubordination are typically very brief and relate to the two forms of insubordination just described. For example, one restaurant chain states that the following cannot be tolerated: "Failure to carry out any order by a management representative, including refusal to do assigned work, and other acts of insubordination." Similarly, a major theme park states that employees are subject to discipline (which could include dismissal without prior warning) for "failure to follow the instructions of your supervisor." A large hospital states that employees are subject to termination on the first offense for insubordination: "disrespect and/or disobedience to authority or deliberate refusal to obey directions of the supervisor." Finally, a large hotel chain classifies insubordination as gross misconduct and states that it could result in termination without previous warning, even if the probationary period is over. It defines insubordination as "failure to carry out a reasonable job assignment or job request of management after being warned that failure to do so can result in termination."

REFUSAL TO OBEY ORDERS

The general rule in industry is that employees have an obligation to obey a legitimate order unless it would be unsafe to do so. They are to do what they are told, even if they do not want to, and may file a grievance later using established channels. In other words, firms are not debating societies; supervisor's requests must be carried out.

Consider the case of the Jamaica Water Supply Company, wherein a field meter repair technician received a work assignment to "upgrade pit" but did not do so. The next day the employee was given a second written work assignment ticket for the same job and was verbally told what was written on the ticket, namely, to make it his first stop and to "upgrade the pit." The employee was told to pick up the material for the job from the meter program yard. Once again the employee disobeyed. He left the yard without getting the needed materials and did not make a stop to upgrade the pit. In his defense the employee argued that this was not a part of his job duties. The arbitrator ruled that the employee was guilty of insubordination and deserved the suspension given by the firm. She argued that employees do not have the right to pick and choose those directions they will follow and those they will not. Employees have an obligation to do what they are told and to follow the contractual provisions for the resolutions of disputes.[1]

In a second case an employee refused a request to move her car, which was parked in a restricted area of the firm's parking lot. She was issued a ticket by the safety manager but refused to accept the ticket. At this point she was asked to accompany the manager to the associate manager's office, but once again she refused. When the company suspended the employee for insubordination, she filed a grievance. The arbitrator ruled that an employee has the obligation to follow an order and then turn to the grievance procedure for further relief. He concluded that the employee's "open deviance" and "air of insubordination" constituted just cause for discipline.[2]

In another case an employee at Washington Hospital Center was ordered to report to the supervisor at the beginning and end of the shift but repeatedly refused on the grounds that the request was unreasonable and discriminatory because it applied only to his department. The arbitrator ruled that the discharge was warranted because the employee had an obligation not to flout the rule.[3]

Although these cases illustrate the basic insubordination principles, others can provide valuable insights into the intricacies of how to give and not give orders. Think of these as the "do's" and "don'ts" of giving effective orders.

Give Valid and Reasonable Work Orders

Orders given by a manager should serve legitimate business purposes. An interesting case that focused on this issue (that of Kilsby Tubesupply, Inc.) involved a supervisor who ordered an employee to sign a time card that the supervisor had altered. In this situation, an employee had attended a grievance meeting that started a half hour before the end of the shift and lasted two hours. He clocked out at the end of the meeting, but the supervisor changed the worker's time card to reflect the time he had stopped working rather than the time he left work. The employee refused to sign the altered card and was suspended for insubordination. The arbitrator in this case ruled that the manager's order "served no legitimate business purpose and did not constitute a valid work order." Therefore, the employee could not be guilty of insubordination. Furthermore, the arbitrator stated that the firm was free to calculate the worker's pay in any way it desired, regardless of whether the employee signed the time card.[4] Not only must work orders be valid, but they must be reasonable. At a Berger Steel fabricating plant, renovation was taking place during the winter so the heat was turned off. Employees were told to work in the plant although the temperature had dipped down to 20 degrees. They refused and were suspended. The arbitrator ruled that the workers should not have been suspended because the order was unreasonable.[5] In another case (that of Ideal Cement Co.), a sixty-year-old employee was discharged for violating a rule prohibiting workers from sitting down during their working hours. The arbitrator concluded, "The no-sit-down rule in a cement plant where operations are at least semi-automatic and therefore to an extent monotonous, temperatures at least at some spots above normal, and floors hard, would seem to go beyond the bounds of reason."[6]

Make Sure Order and Consequences Are Clear

Several basic principles relate to how a manager should communicate orders. One is that employees should clearly understand that an order has been given. In this regard it is important to distinguish between observations, requests, and orders. Consider the following statements made by a supervisor to an employee and determine if any of them constitutes an order:

1. "The floor sure is dirty."
2. "It sure would be nice if the floor were cleaned."
3. "I want you to mop the floor today before lunch."

The first statement could easily be interpreted as an observation, because the manager is making a statement of fact and does not ask anything specific of the employee. Is it also an order? Probably not, unless the manager and employee both know that this is the established way the manager gives orders.

The second statement could be construed as a request because it expresses the manager's preferences or wishes. But is it also an order? Perhaps so; but, once again, it is debatable and would depend on past practice.

Only the third statement is clearly an order. The manager has stated the task to be performed and a timetable has been established.

The important point is this: although employees have an obligation to follow orders, managers have an obligation to be clear regarding which statements are orders and which are not. Telling an employee specifically what needs to be done and when to do it should suffice. However, another approach is to tell the employee that you are giving an order (as is done in the military, i.e., "this is an order"). Still another technique is to tell the employee what the disciplinary consequences will be if the instructions are not carried out (i.e., "If you don't mop the floor, it will constitute insubordination and I will give you a written warning").

It is also important for managers to give clear orders so that employees know exactly what needs to be done. A solid defense against being disciplined for insubordination is that the order was unclear. How clear does it need to be? Enough so that no reasonable person could have misunderstood it.

Finally, managers should tell employees what the penalty may be if they refuse to follow an order. For example, consider the case of an adjuster who was assigned production work but refused. When the company took disciplinary action for insubordination, the employee filed a grievance and it went to arbitration. There was little doubt that the employee had refused an order to perform production work on the night in question, so the arbitrator's decision should seem obvious. Yet, after reviewing the facts, the arbitrator concluded that the employee had a language difficulty and may not have understood the order and the disciplinary warning he was given. He stated that the company appeared to be deficient in making sure that the employee clearly understood both of these as well as the implications of his refusal. The grievance was upheld and the employee was reinstated.[7]

Avoid Orders That Involve Hazards

The major exception to the "obey now, grieve later" principle arises when employees have reasonable cause to believe that the work ordered will be hazardous and unusually dangerous. This exception stems from the Occupational Safety and Health Act of 1970, which states that firms cannot discipline an employee for failure to perform an unsafe act. By the same token, the Taft-Hartley Act of 1947 states that quitting work in good faith because of abnormally dangerous conditions does not constitute a strike. Two practical issues affecting managers on a day-to-day basis arise in this regard.

First, who decides whether a task is too hazardous, the manager or the employee? Most arbitrators maintain that an employee is protected in refusing to perform work, even if in actuality conditions are safe, as long as he/she honestly believes that the situation is dangerous. For example, in the case of A. M. Castle the arbitrator stated that an employee should not be disciplined if he/she is "sincere in his or her belief of danger and so long as he or she makes a reasonable appraisal of the potential hazards."[8]

Several other cases illustrate this point. In the case of Hercules, Inc., the firm discharged an electrician for insubordination because he refused to throw two high voltage switches unless another electrician was present. Management contended that those who refuse to obey an order must demonstrate that a danger actually exists. The arbitrator reinstated the employee and stressed that the employee's fear was "real" enough.[9] In another case (that of Georgia Pacific Corp.) a worker was suspended after refusing to operate a vehicle he believed was in unsafe condition. Finding that the worker's behavior was based on a legitimate concern for his personal safety, the arbitrator decided that the suspension was unjust.[10] In a third case a pipe fitter who was also a member of the firm's safety committee received a five-day suspension for refusing to move parts from one building to another because he believed that the assignment posed a potential hazard to his health. While doing the assigned task one day for the first time, the employee noticed that pigeon droppings were on the parts and all over the working area. When he realized that he was to be assigned to move parts again the next day, he immediately objected and requested that he be reassigned for health reasons. His request was not granted, however, and he was told to move parts. He refused, was suspended, and immediately went to his physician and obtained a release stating that he was to have surgery in one week and "should not be exposed to any hazardous or fecal material that will affect his lungs." The arbitrator ultimately concluded that the employee should not have been suspended because "it was reasonable for him to believe that this health would be jeopardized if he performed the work in question."[11]

Second, can an employee refuse to do work that is uncomfortable but not hazardous? Take the case of employees at National Steel and Shipbuilding Co., who were told to use portable commodes but objected on the basis of safety and health, stating that it was unpleasant to use such facilities without the benefit of hot and cold running water. The arbitrator ruled that although the commodes may have been uncomfortable, they were not a serious threat to the safety and health of employees because there was no evidence that the toilets themselves were unsanitary. The proper method of securing relief would have been to file a grievance or request permission to leave.[12]

In another situation (that of Scripto, Inc.) a woman was terminated for moving her work station away from the noisy area of the plant. The supervisor had ordered her to remain until she substantiated her reported nervous condition with a doctor's slip. She repeatedly disobeyed and ignored a warning that she would be terminated. The arbitrator found no serious health hazard and upheld the termination.[13]

Determining Penalties for Disobeying Orders

The process used to determine the penalty for disobeying orders is similar to that used in determining penalties for other rule infractions. A manager needs to consider the severity of the offense, the employee's work record (job performance, length of service, prior disciplinary record), and any mitigating circumstances that surround the incident. Managers also need to meet the other just cause requirements such as being consistent, having sufficient proof, and so on.

The importance of considering mitigating circumstances was pointed out in the case of a Chesapeake, Virginia, fire fighter who was discharged for insubordination. Lt. Massey arrived at a fire scene that all involved described as chaotic. Four of the ten occupants of a house were at home when grease caught fire on a stove. Neighbors told Lt. Massey that some children remained in the burning house. One neighbor pulled a coat over his head, preparing to enter the blazing building. Instead, Massey and his fellow fire fighters entered. But there was one problem. Lt. Massey had been told by his chief to "stand by" the side of the house because all occupants were safely out of the house. In discharging Lt. Massey, the chief stated that only the commanding officers at fire scenes should make tactical decisions. They, not individual fire fighters on the line, have the most complete information. In addition, it was argued that Lt. Massey's behavior resulted in increased probability of deaths and injuries to both citizens and fire fighters alike. The case was appealed to a panel, which concluded that Massey should receive a ten-day suspension but not be discharged. The panel was of the opinion that "a lack of communications and Lt. Massey's perception of a life-threatening situation sufficiently mitigated the independent actions."[14]

The consistency of punishment is often an issue in insubordination situations. Consider the case of a driver–sales representative for Premium Distributors, Inc., who was discharged for refusing to serve additional stops not on his regularly assigned route. In deciding the case, the arbitrator found that the situation was identical to a previous one involving another employee in which the firm had issued a five-day suspension. Once the arbitrator realized this, he required that the firm reinstate the driver and reduce the punishment to a five-day suspension.[15]

Cases such as these are important because they reinforce the point that insubordinate behaviors do not take place in a vacuum; there are usually previous cases of insubordination and there are always other events surrounding any given insubordinate act. Thus, in determining the appropriate penalty, managers need to evaluate what led up to the act, what the behavior was, and what happened after it occurred, in addition to looking at past precedents.

When an employee does not obey a direct order, a critical consideration is whether this behavior constitutes what is known as gross insubordination. Such behavior is of an outrageous nature and is generally considered to constitute cause for immediate discharge. Even though the behaviors that fall within this category cannot be clearly defined, when an employee flatly refuses to obey a direct order and the refusal is accompanied by threats, violence, or abusive and/or obscene language, a strong case for gross insubordination can be made. In the absence of a strong case, a manager may be able to charge an employee with a lesser charge of insubordination.

The issue of whether an employee had committed gross insubordination was central in a case involving a packer at Astro-Valcour, a manufacturer of plastic packaging material in Massachusetts. One day the firm was short of help, so the packer was assigned to work on a grinding machine. The machine was working improperly and the employee complained that excessive dust was affecting her breathing. After one hour, she was replaced by another employee and reassigned to her regular job. About one hour later, the supervisor asked her if she was ill and planned to leave. She responded affirmatively to both questions and left at noon. The next morning the employee returned to work and found her time card missing from the rack. She approached her supervisor and was told she could not punch in without a medical excuse. Even though she had none, she nonetheless obtained her time card, punched in, and worked all day without further incident. The next day she continued to work, but around 3:00 she was discharged for being insubordinate. She was charged with failing to submit a medical excuse and with telling her boss that it was unnecessary to listen to him and that she was going back to work. In effect, the firm's position was that the employee's behavior constituted gross insubordination. The arbitrator concluded that the employee had an obligation to obey her boss by not returning to work until proper medical clearance had been obtained and subsequently seeking a remedy through the grievance procedure. However, he also concluded that the employee's behavior represented a minor form of insubordination, not gross insubordination; therefore a one-day suspension was the appropriate penalty.[16]

ASSAULT, THREATS, AND ABUSIVE LANGUAGE

Failing to obey a direct order is one form of employee behavior that constitutes insubordination. Other behaviors fall within this category as well, namely, physical assaults, threats of assault on supervision, and abusive language directed at superiors.

Physical Assaults

Assaulting a supervisor is usually considered to be an insubordinate act, but there are some exceptions and intricacies that managers need to understand. The general rule is that an assault is considered insubordination if its roots reside within the employer-employee relationship. After all, a manager's ability to direct the work force is predicated on the assumption that employees will exhibit respect.

However, arbitrators have held that employees may be guilty of insubordination even if they did not personally engage in assault. For example, two employees at Murry Machinery, Inc., blocked the exit and refused to intervene in an off-duty assault of the supervisor by other individuals. The arbitrator noted that these employees aided and abetted the attackers by standing by passively, preventing others to come to the supervisor's assistance, and failing to attempt to restrain the attackers. As a result, they were "accomplices to the assault" and deserving of a suspension for insubordination.[17]

Managers need to address a variety of questions in examining this issue. One is whether the assault is work-related or results from a personal dispute. Consider the case of a manager who went to the race track one night and asked one of his employees which horse to bet on in one of the races. For some reason, however, the employee hit the boss. The next day he was disciplined. Was it insubordination? In examining the case, the arbitrator needed to determine what had caused the fight. He found that the manager and employee had had a major argument at work prior to seeing each other at the race track. He concluded that this caused the assault to occur, that the fight therefore was work-related and stemmed from the employee-employer relationship, and that the employee was guilty of insubordination. On the other hand, if a boss and employee are playing football at a park and during the game the two get into a fight over a tackle, it would not be considered insubordination.

Another question is whether a particular employee behavior constitutes assault or is merely horseplay. In judging these cases the employee's intent is the critical issue. Does the act jeopardize the respect, consideration, and loyalty that a supervisor needs in order to function on the job? In one case (that of Tyrone Hydraulics, Inc.) an employee kicked a supervisor who had bent over to pick up an object on the floor. The employee was discharged for insubordination. Upon examining the case, the arbitrator found that there was much "playing around" at the work site and that the atmosphere was relaxed. He concluded that the kick represented a "spontaneous kind of horseplay without malice or evil intent or any feeling of animosity or anger." He added that a "playful kick can be a compliment among friends."[18]

Another issue is whether an employee who becomes involved in a fight with his/her supervisor is merely engaging in self-defense. Employees cannot be charged with assault if they do nothing more than protect themselves. For example, at Southern Iron and Equipment Co. an employee was discharged for fighting with his supervisor. The arbitrator stated that even though the supervisor may have thrown the first punch, the employee had exceeded his right to self-defense by chasing the supervisor with a piece of iron after the fight had ended. As a result, more than self-defense was involved and the discharge was upheld.[19]

Yet another issue involves determining the appropriate penalty. Assaults are considered a very serious infraction and often warrant discharge. In deciding the penalty, a manager must consider the severity of the act, the employee's work record, and any mitigating circumstances. Often it is helpful to begin the process by looking at the type and nature of the assault committed, the degree of violence involved, who started or provoked the fight, who threw the first punch, and to what extent the employee as opposed to the supervisor was the aggressor. Keep in mind that managers are always free to file suit in civil court charging employees with assault and battery.

Threats of Assault

The threat of assault is usually viewed as a serious infraction, although not as serious as an actual assault. When an employee makes a threat, it undermines the ability of managers to direct workers, particularly if the threat is made in the presence of others. Consider the case of an employee at Narley Cooling Tower Co. who was assigned the task of picking up dog manure. In response, he dumped the manure on the supervisor's desk, broke the supervisor's office window with a steel pipe, and threatened to break open the supervisor's head. The arbitrator sustained the employee's termination and argued that three serious offenses in succession had been committed, each of which merited dismissal.[20] Note that in this case the threats were not just of a verbal nature. Dumping the manure and breaking the window also constituted a threat.

An important consideration is the intent behind a verbal threat. Occasionally, employees may joke around with their boss and say things like, "I'll get even with you for this job assignment." If these statements are made strictly in jest, then no insubordination exists. On the other hand, if the statements are made in an intimidating manner, it does. In a case in point (that of United Parcel Service), a worker raised his fist and told the supervisor to "lay off me, boy, or I'm going to beat your ass." The arbitrator concluded that management was correct in discharging the employee because his words "certainly promised physical harm if the supervisor did not modify his behavior to comply."[21] In another case an employee threatened, in the presence of others, to have his supervisor killed by a hired assassin. The arbitrator upheld the discharge decision because the employee's statements had a "chilling effect on the entire work force" and because if such behavior was condoned, other employees would be more likely to behave similarly.[22]

Although the penalty for threatening one's supervisor is often discharge, a manager must consider the severity of the offense, the employee's work record, and various mitigating circumstances. Whether other employees heard the threat is an important consideration in determining the severity of the act, because such behavior potentially undermines the supervisor's authority. Another important mitigating circumstance is whether, and to what extent, the employee was provoked into the threat by the supervisor. Keep in mind that threats, like other forms of misconduct, may result from actions taken by supervisors. Even though employees are never justified in threatening anyone, a manager's provocation can mitigate the penalty.

Abusive Language/Disparaging Remarks

Abusive language, name calling, derogatory remarks, and back talk can be considered insubordination if they are used to embarrass, ridicule, or degrade a manager. Consider the case of a store clerk in a Safeway Stores supermarket located in Clarksdale, Mississippi, who had worked for the firm for fifteen years. One day the firm received two checks written by the employee that were returned for insufficient funds. The manager attempted to issue a written warning to the employee, but he refused to accept the warning. The next day the manager attempted to meet with the employee, but the employee refused to come to the meeting. Later the manager heard the employee call to him from the front of the store. When the manager got there the employee unleashed a verbal assault and said he would "call the man" and "shut down the store." He added that "one of us will be gone by Monday." All this shouting occurred in front of employees, customers, and vendors. The employee was terminated for insubordination. In this case the arbitrator agreed with the firm's decision, stating that the employee's behavior constituted gross insubordination on account of its belittling effect on the supervisor, impeding the supervisor's ability to function properly.[23]

Still, in many work settings (e.g., in the construction industry) profane language is common among employees, including supervisors. The friendly use of this language is often considered "shop-talk." Nevertheless, when such language is intended to demean or belittle a manager it becomes insubordination. The question of intent then becomes important, not the words themselves. In the case of Paragon Bridge and Steel Co., an employee told the supervisor to go f___ himself. The supervisor informed the employee that he would be given a warning for such language and started to walk away. The employee called after him and repeated the remark in the presence of other employees. The arbitrator upheld the employee's discharge, arguing that the employee had clearly intended to degrade and ridicule the manager. He added that the firm must maintain employee respect of supervision and that it cannot condone repeated insubordination without losing this respect.[24]

Calling a supervisor names or saying that he/she is "a liar" constitutes insubordination whenever the intent is to degrade the supervisor or undermine his/her ability to manage the work force. However, name-calling done in a friendly, joking manner would not be cause for discipline. In one case an employee told his boss that he was a "damned liar." Here the arbitrator reduced the penalty because of the employee's past good work record and because no other employees heard the remark.[25]

In many firms it is fairly common for employees to grumble when given a job assignment and to cast disparaging remarks regarding supervision, pointing out what "jerks" all supervisors are. Whether the manager can take disciplinary action in these cases is often unclear because of the fact that employees have the constitutional right of free speech, or what has been termed "healthy griping." In the case of back-talking, a manager would be wise to warn the employee that his/her patience is running out and that disciplinary action will be forthcoming if the grumbling doesn't stop. A case in point concerned an employee at Armour Agricultural Chemical Co. with twenty years of experience who continuously grumbled when given an order. This included statements like, "I know my job." At one point the manager finally had enough and fired the employee. The arbitrator reduced the discharge to a suspension because he viewed the action as being too drastic, given the fact that the company had tolerated the employee's grumbling for twenty years and had not taken strong disciplinary action.[26]

The most difficult situation faced by a manager is when employees make critical remarks regarding the manager or other members of management. Obviously, most managers do not like employees to do this. However, because employees do have the right to free speech that is not slanderous, such remarks are not usually considered grounds for disciplinary action even if the supervisor overhears them. Before considering disciplinary action, a manager should consider whether the statements were malicious in character and whether they had a significant effect on the morale and productivity of other employees.

Is Whistle-Blowing Insubordination?

A person who reports a real or perceived wrong done by his or her employer is called a whistle-blower. Is this insubordination, particularly if management has told employees not to tell anyone about an incident or situation?

Whistle-blowing is protected under various laws. However, rights to free speech are not protected by a comprehensive whistle-blowing law that applies to both public and private employees. At present, whistle-blowers who work in civil service systems have more protection than those who work in private industry.

CONCLUSION

This chapter has focused on the topic of insubordination, one of the most difficult disciplinary issues facing managers. In a sense, insubordination is the most overriding of all work rules. All these rules are written in the form of do's and don'ts (e.g., do wear safety glasses, do be at work promptly at 8:00 A.M., don't sleep on the job, don't steal company property) and therefore could be considered direct orders. Thus, when an employee breaks any rule, one could argue that the employee is simultaneously guilty of insubordination.

Unfortunately, many employees and managers have at best only a vague understanding of what behaviors constitute insubordination. Thus, although almost all firms have a policy stating that employees cannot be insubordinate, few really know what this means operationally. In this chapter we have defined the term to include four specific behaviors: refusal to obey orders, physical assaults on superiors, threats of assault directed toward supervisors, and directing abusive language and derogatory remarks toward managers. However, there is no law or rule that limits insubordination to these four behaviors. Indeed, some firms have defined the term to include only the refusal to obey orders. But most arbitrators and firms define it more broadly.

In terms of dealing with insubordination, various arbitration cases have established certain basic principles. Managers have a responsibility to give clear, valid, and reasonable orders that serve legitimate business purposes. Employees have an obligation to follow orders unless they are being asked to perform an unsafe act. If an employee refuses a legitimate order, the appropriate penalty depends upon the severity of the offense, the person's past work and disciplinary record, and any mitigating circumstances surrounding the incident.

NOTES

1. Jamaica Water Supply Co., 90 LA 8040.
2. Federal Correction Institution, 75 LA 295.
3. Washington Hospital Center, 75 LA 32.
4. Kilsby Tubesupply, Inc., 76 LA 921.
5. Berger Steel Co., 46 LA 1131.
6. Ideal Cement Co., 13 LA 943.
7. 89-1 ARB 8018.
8. A. M. Castle & Co., 41 LA 666.
9. Hercules, Inc., 48 LA 788.
10. Georgia Pacific Corp., 76 LA 808.
11. Al Tech Specialty Steel Corp., 91 LA 8153.
12. National Steel and Shipbuilding Co., 64 LA 466.
13. Scripto, Inc., 48 LA 980.

14. The *Virginian Pilot and the Ledger Star*, August 20, 1990.
15. 89-1 ARB 8034.
16. Astro-Valcour, Inc., 89 LA 8545.
17. Murry Machinery, Inc., 75 LA 284.
18. Tyrone Hydraulics, Inc., 75 LA 672.
19. Southern Iron & Equipment Co., 65 LA 694.
20. Narley Cooling Tower Co., 66 LA 325.
21. United Parcel Service, Inc., 76 LA 1086.
22. Protective Treatments, Inc., 61 LA 1292.
23. Safeway Stores, Inc., 87 LA 8397.
24. Paragon Bridge and Steel Co., 43 LA 864.
25. Higgins Industries, Inc., 25 LA 439.
26. Armour Agricultural Chemical Co., 40 LA 289.

Chapter 5

Reducing Employee Theft and Dishonesty

As he was leaving the fast-food restaurant "East and Easy" in Warren, Michigan, an employee was approached by his supervisor, who had observed him hiding a six-ounce can of orange juice under his coat. After he was stopped, the employee dropped the juice on the floor and left the premises. The next day, when approached by management regarding the incident, the employee denied that he had attempted to steal the juice. The employee was fired and filed a grievance. The union maintained that the company had failed to establish "beyond a reasonable doubt" that the grievant had stolen the juice or even seen the container on the floor. Although the grievant was a low-seniority employee with a poor disciplinary record, the union argued that it was improper to discharge him on account of theft.[1]

How should a situation such as this be handled? Clearly, the employee was attempting to steal the juice. On the other hand, the value of the item was nominal and trivial. The employee was not engaged in embezzlement or major theft of company property that could be used or sold to others. Doesn't it seem that immediate discharge is a bit severe in this case?

As it turns out, the arbitrator found that the discharge was reasonable. According to his ruling, "Pilferage of company property by one, or several employees, jeopardizes the employment security of all other employees of the company. The employer has established and maintained its business for the purpose of making a profit. Stealing goods that otherwise would be sold, diminishes the possibility that the company will make a profit . . . [and] reduces the chance of maintaining the enterprise. . . . It is in the interest of the company, the union, and all employees to prohibit and/or eliminate the swiping of company property."[2]

In a sense, however, the items stolen are not the whole story. When employees engage in this kind of behavior they have violated a basic tenet of the employer-employee relationship, that being trust. If someone steals from the company that pays his/her salary, the person can no longer be trusted; once trust is lost, the employer has no choice but to fire the individual.

In this chapter we examine various issues related to employee theft and dishonesty. We discuss different situations in which theft occurs, examine the question of mitigating circumstances, look at options for combating theft, and consider the legal issues surrounding employee investigations.

NATURE OF THE PROBLEM

Many corporations have long recognized the value of loss-prevention programs, but there is little indication that American companies are effectively combating theft and dishonesty in the workplace. Although it is difficult to find consistent data, it is clear that theft and misuse of company equipment pose tremendous costs on employers. The Bureau of National Affairs estimates that business losses from employee dishonesty run between $15 billion and $20 billion a year. The U.S. Chamber of Commerce says that losses total $40 billion a year. In his book, *Reducing Employee Theft*, Neil Snyder agrees with the Chamber's estimate and predicts increasing costs at an alarming 15 percent per year. He also believes that one-third of all business failures are attributable to employee dishonesty.[3]

To make matters worse, employee dishonesty and theft are not due to "a few bad apples." In a survey of 9,000 industrial employees, fully 30 percent of the subjects admitted having stolen from their employers. In 1988 the *Wall Street Journal* reported that up to 75 percent of all employees steal at least once, and half of these steal twice.[4] In fact, internal theft in many retail firms causes far greater losses than does shoplifting.

In an effort to combat theft and dishonesty, a company can seek outside help. Yet the most effective loss-prevention efforts require the ongoing participation and support of all managers, from the top on down. As a first step, managers need to set a good example. For instance, Reuben Mark of Colgate Palmolive logs and pays for every personal call he makes. Charles Lazarus of Toys 'R' Us—who says, "Honesty is the only policy"—makes sure that overages as well as shortages are scrupulously accounted for during the receiving process.[5]

DEALING WITH THEFT AND DISHONESTY

Employee dishonesty refers to a willful perversion of the truth in order to deceive, cheat, or fraud. It can take any number of forms, including lying on an application blank and falsifying expense accounts, time, or work records. Theft, on the other hand, is generally recognized as the unauthorized taking, control, or transfer of money and/or property belonging to the employer (or belonging to coworkers on company property) that is perpetrated by an employee during the course of his/her employment.[6] When it is done in small amounts or small values over time, the term "pilferage" or "shrinkage" is often applied.

Most firms that have an employee handbook or formal work rules specify theft and various forms of dishonesty as being expressly forbidden and subjecting the offender to immediate discharge. Exhibit 5.1 provides several typical examples. If no such rules exist, the situation may be more complex; but even here an employer is reasonably entitled to expect honesty on the part of employees. Nevertheless, evidence against the offender must be completely clear and convincing; hearsay and rumor generally are not sufficient.

Most arbitrators believe that employee theft and dishonesty are offenses that warrant summary dismissal; progressive discipline may not be required in these cases. This is especially true when employees are guilty of stealing. There are instances, however, when exceptional circumstances or mitigating factors must be considered. These include the following situations: (1) the company condones or is in some way involved in the dishonest behavior; (2) the company discharges an employee for off-duty theft or dishonesty that has no connection to the employee's job; (3) the person may be considered to be disabled from alcohol or drug abuse; or (4) the employee has a long, unblemished work record and the theft or dishonest behavior is not especially severe from the company's point of view.

In other words, arbitrators and managers need to consider all the circumstances, especially given the severe stigma attached to employees who are discharged for theft and/or dishonesty. For example, in *American Welding and Manufacturing Co.* the arbitrator wrote:[7]

There is practically no category of misconduct which automatically justifies employee termination. Every employee faced with discipline is entitled to judicious consideration of individual mitigating factors. Of course, some offenses are more serious than others and most likely to justify discharge. Generally, stealing from an employer is so contrary to an employee's responsibilities that it literally cancels the employment relationship. Only in exceptional circumstances will an arbitrator reverse an employer's decision to fire a proven thief. But even a thief is entitled to thorough examination of mitigating factors.

Company Condones Conduct

When an employee is charged with theft or misuse of company property but in the past the company has condoned the practice or is in some way involved, arbitrators frequently find that summary discharge is inappropriate. For example, in an incident involving the Carnation Company, the

Exhibit 5.1
Theft/Dishonesty Policies

POLICY EXCERPT #1: The following offenses are considered serious enough to warrant immediate suspension and normally discharge:

— Theft, misappropriation or willful destruction of company or other employees' property.

— Falsification of records, reports, time cards, vouchers, etc., including application for employment.

POLICY EXCERPT #2: Employees are cautioned that they may be subject to disciplinary action for violation of the following rules:

— Unexcused failure to ring clock or otherwise record time in or out.

First Offense: Written reprimand

Second Offense: 2-day suspension

Third Offense: 3-day suspension to termination

Reckoning period two (2) years

— Ring clock or otherwise record time in or out for another employee, or to permit an unauthorized employee to ring clock or otherwise record time in or out for oneself; or falsifying attendance record for oneself or for another employee; or for permitting another employee to falsify one's attendance record.

First Offense: Written reprimand to 1-day suspension

Second Offense: 2-day suspension to 5-day suspension

Third Offense: 5-day suspension to termination of employment.

Reckoning period two (2) years

— Actual or attempted taking and carrying away government property or the property of others.

First Offense: Written reprimand to termination of employment

Second Offense: Termination of employment

Reckoning period two (2) years

POLICY EXCERPT #3: The following acts or conduct are prohibited:

— Giving food away. (You may be under pressure to give food to friends who visit your restaurant. This is strictly forbidden and grounds for immediate termination. Do not jeopardize your future here or with other employers by "playing the role".)

— Unauthorized access to restricted areas, property or records or removing from restaurant premises without proper written authorization, restaurant property, including food, records or other materials, or removing from restaurant premises without proper authorization the property of customer or fellow employees.

Exhibit 5.1 (continued)

—Falsification of application for employment or any other restaurant
records or documents.

—Falsely stating or making claims of injury.

—Not punching time card, or punching another's time card, or falsifying
or altering a time card in any manner.

---

firm discharged a union steward for the theft of fourteen pads of paper
that he obtained without authorization from a company supply room. The
arbitrator ruled that the discharge was inappropriate because in the past
the employer had generally ignored and thus condoned the practice of
union stewards taking office supplies from the storeroom. Besides, the
steward did not take the pads for his personal use. Because he intended
to use them for an official company-union conference, he did not need
official authorization.[8]

Consider the case of Vulcan Materials, in which a manager discharged
an employee for falsifying log books in order to cover up an accident.
During arbitration the grievant was found guilty of deliberately falsifying
an official company record. However, because the arbitrator determined
that the company had condoned the falsification of log books in the past
and had not dismissed other guilty drivers, the discharge was reduced to
a suspension. The arbitrator stated that "falsification of log books, lies,
and other violations of company regulations must be treated uniformly."[9]
By enforcing theft/dishonesty policies in some cases but not others, employers run the risk that discharge penalties will be reduced or overturned.

Off-Duty Misconduct

Cases involving an employee arrested for theft while off duty can present special problems for managers. Generally, there are two separate but
interrelated issues. One is the effect of the behavior on the employer's
business or reputation. The other is whether the alleged misconduct warrants a severe penalty.

Normally in grievance arbitration involving off-duty misconduct, the actions and findings of a court do not have a directing influence on the case
nor do they determine the arbitrator's ruling. Rather, employers are generally required to prove that the misconduct is significantly related to on-
the-job considerations. In other words, the firm must establish a nexus
between the alleged conduct and some legitimate facet of the employer's
business—such as being injurious to the firm's reputation or its product,

or the incident rendering the employee incapable of performing his/her job at the same level of competency.[10] Similarly, in a case involving a route driver for Means Services Inc., the arbitrator held that the penalty of discharge was too severe even though the employee had pleaded guilty to theft while off duty. Although the arbitrator noted that theft of any kind raises serious doubts about an employee's trustworthiness, the evidence of the employee's conviction did not establish that the grievant's ability to perform his job competently was impaired or that the business was directly or adversely affected.[11]

In addition to requiring that a nexus be shown, many arbitrators apply the "beyond a reasonable doubt" standard of proof when deciding off-duty theft cases. For example, in a recent unpublished award, one arbitrator reinstated an employee who was discharged for shoplifting while off duty. The employer, a food retailer, argued that it had a long-standing practice of discharging employees for serious off-duty misconduct because such conduct affects the company. In this case the arbitrator overturned the discharge on the grounds that the employer's investigation of the alleged off-duty theft was not thorough and that there was insufficient evidence that the employee stole anything.

Circumstances Related to Alcohol and Drug Abuse

Arguing that one is impaired by alcohol and drug abuse can mitigate a discharge for theft, depending on the arbitrator. Some do not believe substance abuse should be considered, but others do, especially when the employee has a long tenure on the job, his/her work record is good, and the severity of the abuse problem does not seem overwhelming. In addition, some consider whether the employer has an established Employee Assistance Program and whether the employee has been asked to participate in the program in lieu of immediate discharge. Yet, even if the impairment is considered a valid mitigating circumstance, reinstatement of a discharged employee is almost always conditional on the person's willingness to seek help from an established alcohol or drug treatment program.[12]

Work Record as a Mitigating Circumstance

Finally, a long and unblemished work record can work to the advantage of someone accused of theft or dishonesty. For example, at Kroger Company a journeyman meat cutter was discharged for removing a 67-cent bag of peanuts from its display peg in a retail store. The arbitrator felt that this was not justified and ordered the employee to be reinstated without back pay: "In view of all the circumstances, the discharge of an employee who has given his continuous service to a company for twenty-three years for eating a handful of nuts is simply too severe. Although the grievant's actions cannot be condoned . . . the grievant's action does not warrant the degree of discipline imposed."[13]

The fact that management should consider an employee's work record if it does not want the discharge decision to be overturned is reinforced by an arbitration case involving Standard Oil of Ohio. In this situation an employee was discharged for removing refinery equipment from company property, but the arbitrator ruled that the evidence was not sufficient to justify such a severe penalty. The grievant had a good work record, with only a single one-day suspension in over eight years. There was also no evidence during his employment that he was dishonest. When these facts were taken into consideration, the grievance was sustained.[14]

On the other hand, an arbitrator might be inclined to uphold a discharge if the past record included discipline for alleged dishonesty. The best advice for a manager is to consider the employee's past work history before taking severe disciplinary actions.

How Much Proof?

Having considered various mitigating circumstances, how much proof does a manager need before taking action? It is a well-established principle that because discharge is the ultimate penalty, the employer must carry a heavy burden in supporting its actions. In cases involving employee theft, some arbitrators require clear and convincing evidence of the employee's guilt, whereas others hold that proof must be beyond a reasonable doubt. In any event, when the decision to fire is based on evidence that is hearsay or contradictory, the employer's actions are frequently reversed.

Quite often, arbitrators are presented with only circumstantial evidence in theft cases rather than direct evidence or eyewitness accounts. Using criminal law standards for guidance, the arbitrator in the case of General Telephone Company of Southwest took the position that "circumstances relied upon must be consistent with the theory of guilt and inconsistent with any reasonable theory of innocence." In this case it was ruled that suspicions alone are not enough to support a discharge. Because the employer had failed to show an intent to steal a teledialer and there was only inconclusive, circumstantial evidence to support the discharge, the grievance was upheld.[15] Beyond clear and convincing facts, arbitrators usually require evidence of an employee's intent to steal company property or to act in a dishonest manner before upholding a discharge. Again, the burden of proof rests squarely with the company. For example, in cases in which an employee is accused of falsifying company records, the most crucial factor is proof of intent to pervert the truth in order to deceive, cheat, or fraud.

Most arbitrators also believe they have a duty to safeguard the interests of the discharged employee by making reasonably sure that the penalty imposed is just and equitable and that other fair-minded persons would believe that the offense warrants a discharge. The arbitrator attempts to determine an employee's guilt and at the same time considers whether the employer acted in an arbitrary, capricious, or unreasonable manner. If an employer seems to be treating one employee in a way that is clearly different from other employees found guilty of the same offense, the discharge may well be reduced to a suspension.[16]

Therefore, a manager has a responsibility to treat all employees fairly and consistently in cases of theft or dishonesty. For example, if a manager suspects problems but looks the other way for a time with some employees but not others, any decision to suddenly discharge an employee may well be viewed as unfair treatment and the grievance is likely to be sustained.

COMBATING EMPLOYEE THEFT

To prevent theft and dishonest acts, as well as to minimize the costs, firms have tried a number of different devices and methods. These include polygraphs, paper-and-pencil honesty tests, power interviews, workplace monitoring, and employee searches.

Use of Polygraphs

The Employee Polygraph Protection Act of 1988 severely limits the use of polygraph examinations by prohibiting private employers from requesting that job applicants and/or current employees submit to a lie detector exam except under certain narrowly defined circumstances, one of which is an ongoing investigation involving theft or economic loss. Even in this situation there are several limitations. For example, reasonable suspicion must be established in a written statement given to the employee prior to the test. According to the law, the statement must: (1) describe the investigation and reason for testing; (2) point out that the employee had access to the property under investigation; (3) establish a basis of reasonable suspicion; and (4) list the questions to be asked. In addition, an employee may refuse to take the test or stop in the middle, and this cannot be construed as an admission of guilt.[17]

These restrictions created by the act have limited not only the use but also the effectiveness of this particular tool. In fact, under some circumstances, asking an employee to submit to a polygraph may create additional liability for an employer. Even if the manager has an abundance of other information indicating an employee's guilt, a person who refuses to take a polygraph exam may be able to claim that he/she was subsequently discharged only because of a refusal to take the test.

Paper-and-Pencil Honesty Tests

Paper-and-pencil honesty tests have become increasingly popular, because these devices are not prohibited by the Employee Polygraph Protection Act and therefore provide firms with a reasonable alternative method of determining who is likely to engage in theft. Most commercially available instruments are designed to inquire into an employee's attitudes toward theft and other forms of dishonesty. Common areas of inquiry include the following: (1) beliefs about the frequency and extent of theft in our society (e.g., "What percentage of people take more than $1.00 per week from their employer?"); (2) punitiveness toward theft (e.g., "Should a person be fired if caught stealing $5.00?"); (3) ruminations about theft (e.g., "Have you ever thought about taking company merchandise without actually taking any?"); (4) likelihood of detection (e.g., "What percentage of employee thieves are ever caught?"); (5) knowledge of employee theft (e.g., "Do you know for certain that some of your friends steal from their employer?"); (6) rationalizations about theft (e.g., "An employer who pays people poorly has it coming when employees steal"); and (7) assessment of one's own honesty (e.g., "Compared to other people, how honest are you?").[18]

Some honesty tests claim to disguise their purpose by embedding items such as those just listed among other nonthreatening items (e.g., "Radio, television, and printed news is boring") in an attempt to reduce the possibility of faking. A few actually contain no obvious or direct reference to theft. These tests were developed through the empirical identification of standard personality items that supposedly differentiate between persons known to be dishonest and those assumed to be honest (employees with no record of theft).[19]

Even though honesty tests are more frequently used as a selection device, they can be an option during a theft investigation. As was the case with polygraphs, there are differing views as to the accuracy of honesty tests; and the research that has been done on test validity is far from conclusive. Thus, care should always be taken to ask employees questions that are clearly job-related.[20] Nevertheless, this is a viable option when investigating theft/dishonesty.

Power Interviews

So-called power interviews are used by some employers in connection with employee theft and dishonesty investigations. As with polygraph and honesty tests, power interviews require considerable training; professional investigators tend to be most effective in administering this investigatory tool. Just as there is a direct relationship between the talent and experience of the person administering a polygraph test and successful results, there may be an even greater connection between the ability of the interviewer and the frequency with which the person obtains admissions of employee misconduct.

Although they are not directly affected by state or federal statutes, these interviews can lead to state tort claims if they are not properly administered. For example, extremely forceful or coercive tactics might cause the person to claim intentional infliction of emotional distress.[21]

Workplace Monitoring

A fourth option is to use electronic workplace monitoring as a way of determining who may be involved in theft or other types of dishonest behavior. In some cases this approach not only detects but may also prevent theft, because employees who know or suspect that their actions are being monitored may be less likely to engage in dishonest behaviors. Methods for this type of surveillance include telephone monitoring, computer monitoring, telecopy monitoring, electronic mail monitoring, and video/audio surveillance.

Although these forms of monitoring are generally permitted in most states and there is no universal restriction under federal law, certain types of monitoring may be limited by federal or state wiretap laws. For example, under Title III of the Omnibus Crime Control and Safe Streets Act of 1968, it is illegal to monitor someone's telephone conversations unless the consent of the person has been obtained, and even then the employer cannot monitor personal calls. In addition, monitoring that is unreasonably invasive (e.g., cameras in restrooms) may lead to the filing of lawsuits and arbitration decisions in favor of employees. If the monitoring extends to off-duty activities or leads to negative information becoming public, then defamation and slander lawsuits can result.[22] It is generally argued that activities such as these should be used only in the most extreme situations in which safety, the employer's reputation, or large sums of money are concerned.

Workplace Searches

A controversial method for combating theft and dishonesty involves employee searches in the workplace. Unlike the other measures discussed here, searches of property used by employees bring into question the proper balance between (1) the employer's right to operate its business and implement reasonable work rules, and (2) the privacy rights and interests of employees.

As we have stated throughout this book, the presumed right to privacy is limited as far as the workplace is concerned. The Fourth Amendment only protects one against the actions of government. Thus, unless the employer is government or one is dealing with a private employer doing extensive business with and heavily regulated by the government, there are relatively few restrictions. A private employer has a good deal of latitude, but even here reason must prevail and it would not be wise for any firm to issue open-ended search warrants to all managerial personnel.[23]

The issue in terms of employee searches is whether an individual has a reasonable and legitimate expectation of privacy. As we have noted in other chapters, an employer may search an employee's desk or locker. However, all employees should be properly informed that their work areas/lockers might be searched if there is reasonable suspicion. In most cases it would be wise to state this in the employee handbook and make sure that people are aware of it. In addition, it is often recommended that as part of the pre-employment packet, employers obtain a signed consent to search either desks or lockers (because forced searches of employees can lead to lawsuits and grievances). Keep in mind, however, that an employer may take disciplinary action against employees who refuse to cooperate in an ongoing investigation.[24]

A MANAGER'S ROLE IN PREVENTION

Until now, this chapter has concentrated on what firms can do to control theft. The emphasis here is on attacking the problem through tighter organizational policies, surveillance techniques, and other relatively coercive tactics. In addition, there are a variety of actions that individual managers can take.[25] For example:

- *Define theft and communicate a theft policy.* Managers must determine exactly what constitutes theft. For instance, is using a copier or company telephone for personal business considered theft? How much petty pilferage of supplies is the firm willing to tolerate? Paycheck inserts, company newsletter articles, company training sessions, and so on can all be used to communicate management's concerns and to spell out the consequences if theft is detected.

- *Treat employees with dignity and respect.* If people are treated as honest individuals, research has shown that they will act that way. A healthy organizational climate influences employees directly and fosters norms that discourage theft.

- *Establish non-adversarial relationships with employees.* It is much more difficult to cheat or steal from a friend.

- *Provide reinforcement for non-theft behaviors.* Why be honest if it doesn't pay and there is no reward? Managers can and should establish loss-prevention goals and then reward employees for reaching them. Even though financial rewards are probably inappropriate, positive feedback and praise are not unreasonable.

- *Refer needy employees for assistance.* Supervisors need to be aware of psychological problems, emotional disorders, and substance abuses that develop on the job. Often these problems lead to theft and dishonesty. Employees with such problems should be referred to appropriate professional personnel before they abuse company property or start stealing.

- *Let disgruntled employees vent their anger.* Informal complaint sessions or discussions can be used to relieve frustration. Remember that frustration breeds anger, which leads to theft and other forms of dysfunctional behavior.

- *Provide models of organizational integrity.* Managers can encourage or discourage theft and dishonesty by leading by example. If managers use company equipment in violation of specific rules, employees are likely to do the same. What one does is always more important than what one says.

- *Notify law enforcement officials if major theft is discovered.* When the problem is more than minor pilferage or simple misuse of company equipment, the police should be notified. They are better equipped to investigate theft; besides, this takes a good deal of the burden off the manager by allowing him/her to be somewhat less directly involved.

Clearly, managers play a major role in the theft and dishonesty behaviors of their employees. They need to take an active part in theft prevention instead of assuming that control measures alone will do the job.

LEGAL RAMIFICATIONS OF THEFT INVESTIGATIONS

When investigating allegations of theft or dishonesty, a manager should always be aware of the potential for lawsuits and other legal actions. In addition to charges of discrimination and wrongful discharge (see Chapter 2) there are other common causes for action, including defamation, intentional infliction of emotional distress, and false imprisonment and assault. Although these state torts are not unique to theft investigations, they are likely to be used by employees if managers are too zealous or when the person is discharged or severely sanctioned on the basis of unfounded allegations. To determine any organization's exposure to state tort actions, one would have to examine the laws of each jurisdiction in which the corporation operates. However, the three causes for action noted here are recognized in virtually every state, and they require special attention.

Defamation

During an investigation, employees have a right to expect that their good name and reputation will not be unnecessarily tarnished. It is important to guard against unrestricted dissemination of personal information. Access to information that could be damaging should be restricted to those individuals who have a legitimate need to know. This will reduce the risk of a defamation claim against the employer by employees who feel that something negative about their reputation and good name has been improperly published or stated to a third party. A manager should always be careful to obtain as much information as possible before making accusations, and then only transmit this to appropriate individuals. This should preserve the firm's "conditional privilege" in such matters (see Chapter 2).[26]

The case of *Turnbarella v. Kroger*[27] illustrates the problems that can result from the unnecessarily widespread dissemination of information. A supermarket chain was found liable for both invasion of privacy and defamation after informing all its supervisors that a cashier had been fired for theft. The court found that Kroger's privilege to release this information within the corporation was lost because the disclosure went overboard. The court said that not all of the several dozen supervisors needed to know this information.

Intentional Infliction of Emotional Distress

A second commonly recognized tort is intentional infliction of emotional distress. When it comes to investigations of theft and employee dishonesty, this is a serious concern. Employees often file this claim when they believe that the employer's conduct during an investigation or search was overly aggressive and subjected the person to undue humiliation and mental strain.

Because this is a widely recognized cause for action and because judgments are often substantial, it is important that it be considered at all times. The best rule is to make sure that all investigatory procedures are applied according to a reasonable policy that is well understood by the work force. In addition, an individual's confidentiality should be protected until all the facts have been gathered, and nobody should be subjected to a public interrogation.

False Imprisonment and Assault

By necessity, a search may involve restricting an individual's freedom of movement and unauthorized touching. If this happens, the employee may charge the firm with false imprisonment and/or assault. Again, these violations can be expensive. To make matters even more complex, an unlawful restraint charge can arise not only from direct conduct but also if the words used by company officials when confronting an employee indicate that force may and can be used and the means of coercion are clearly at hand.

For example, in the case of *Johnson v. Pennsylvania Railroad Co.*[28] an employee was accused of stealing food, was searched, and was detained for two hours by private railroad police pending a brief inquiry into the matter. He was told to either sign a confession or face other "serious consequences." He signed the confession and subsequently sued the employer. The court found that he had a valid cause for action because his freedom of movement was restrained in a manner that induced a reasonable apprehension that some force might be used.

Similarly, in *Black v. Kroger Co.*[29] a checkout clerk was accused of stealing from the cash register. Although she was never physically restrained, a jury found that she was sufficiently intimidated to be put in fear of her life, property, or reputation. According to the court, the employee felt she could not leave the room where she was being interviewed by security personnel. The court concluded that the employer unlawfully imprisoned the employee even though she never asked to leave or indicated a desire to terminate the interview.

In addition to false imprisonment, if an employee is physically restrained or if a search of his/her person is conducted the company may find itself faced with a lawsuit charging assault and battery. Essentially, any "unwanted" touch of an employee is suspect and may lead to further problems. Even if there are no lawsuits, unionized employees and many in nonunion firms may respond by filing grievances. For example, in a case involving National Vendors[30] the arbitrator found that the company did not have the right to resort to "self-help" measures when a supervisor tried to force open the hand of an employee suspected of possessing contraband material. The grievance was sustained and the employee reinstated.

CONCLUSION

Employee dishonesty refers to a willful perversion of the truth in order to deceive, cheat, or fraud. Stealing or theft, on the other hand, refers to the taking of property without permission. This behavior results in considerable losses for many organizations each year. In fact, theft by retail employees is a larger problem than shoplifting by customers.

Although most employees are fully aware that they are stealing when they take something of real value, many do not feel they are doing anything wrong when they pilfer items such as pens, pencils, pads, and paper clips. Indeed, many employees consider small amounts of pilferage as a fringe benefit to which they are rightly entitled. This attitude is often sanctioned by managers who look the other way when employees walk out the door with company property or who neglect to implement security measures designed to reduce theft. Managers need to clarify what is considered theft and consistently enforce the rules.

Theft and dishonesty normally lead to the employee being discharged. However, an employee who is tagged with the stigma of being a thief might find it difficult to ever again secure meaningful employment, so arbitrators are generally very careful to examine and weigh the quality and quantity of evidence presented by the employer. Management should be mindful that the burden of proof falls on the employer to justify its actions and that exceptional circumstances may mitigate the penalty. These may include situations in which the company has condoned the behavior; the behavior takes place off duty and there is no discernable nexus to the job; the person is a disabled substance abuser; or the person has a long unblemished work record. When these conditions exist, suspension without pay may be preferable to discharge unless the offense is truly serious.

In an effort to combat theft and dishonesty, firms have used polygraphs; honesty tests; power interviews; electronic monitoring; and searches of desk, lockers, and work areas. All these have an array of legal ramifications and none is a perfect solution. In fact, if employers are too zealous, employees may claim wrongful discharge and/or discrimination. In addition, they may bring legal action under several widely recognized torts, including defamation, intentional infliction of emotional distress, and false imprisonment and assault.

We have argued that managers play an important role in preventing theft and dishonesty. Rather than concentrating on only the "control" approach, managers can be actively involved by setting clear rules, establishing a positive atmosphere, rewarding employees for honesty on the job, and so on. These actions should help to boost morale because employees will be aware that their employer is dealing with them fairly and openly, thereby fostering sound, progressive employee relations.

NOTES

1. American Society of Personnel Administration, *Resource*, March 1988.
2. Ibid.
3. T. B. Kinni, "Lock the Door before the Horse is Stolen," *Industry Week*, May 4, 1992.
4. Ibid.
5. Ibid.
6. C. H. Garbutt and L. E. Stallworth, "Theft in the Workplace: An Arbitrator's Perspective on Employee Discipline," *Arbitrator Journal*, September 1989.
7. Ibid.
8. Ibid.
9. Ibid.
10. M. F. Hill, Jr., and A. Sinicropi, *Management Rights* (Washington, DC: BNA Books Arbitration Series, 1986).
11. Garbutt and Stallworth, "Theft in the Workplace."
12. Ibid.
13. K. Jennings, D. Kare, and A. Goela, "An Analysis of Arbitration Decisions in Employee Theft Cases," *Labor Law Journal*, March 1991.
14. Ibid.
15. Garbutt and Stallworth, "Theft in the Workplace."

16. Ibid.

17. Kaufman and Canoles, "Investigating and Confronting Employee Misconduct," *Employee Law Update*, Conference Proceedings 1993.

18. P. R. Sackett, "Honesty Testing for Personnel Selection," *Personnel Administrator*, September 1985.

19. Ibid.

20. Kaufman and Canoles, "Investigating and Confronting Employee Misconduct."

21. Ibid.

22. Ibid. See also Kruchko and Fries, Counselors at Law, *Employee Relations Newsletter*, December 1992/January 1993.

23. R. J. Nobile, "Employee Searches in the Workplace: Developing a Realistic Policy," *Personnel Administrator*, May 1985.

24. Kaufman and Canoles, "Investigating and Confronting Employee Misconduct."

25. R. R. Taylor, "Your Role in the Prevention of Employee Theft," *Management Solutions*, August 1986.

26. Ibid.

27. Nobile, "Employee Searches in the Workplace."

28. Ibid.

29. Ibid.

30. Ibid.

Chapter 6

Confronting and Controlling Substance Abusers

When the director of industrial relations picks up his ringing telephone, the caller identifies herself only as a forklift driver at a large distribution center who has been with the company for several years. Then she says, "Many of the people I work with are drinking or on drugs, and there are people using or selling drugs at work. I'm frightened, and I don't want to work with them any longer. You have a responsibility to stop it, and if you don't do something now, I'm going to make the same phone call to your boss. If that doesn't work, I'm going to call the police."

This veiled threat gets his attention. Clearly, he doesn't want the matter to go any further. Besides, the company prohibits possession and use of drugs and alcohol while at work and local management should be able to enforce the rules. However, the problem is that up to this time, drug and alcohol use—especially off the job—has been passed off as just an unfortunate sign of the times. Now the times seem to be changing again, and the employee's admonition, "You have a responsibility to stop it," keeps ringing in the director's ears.[1] If you were the director, what would you do?

Unfortunately, this scenario has become increasingly common because individuals do not leave their drug and alcohol problems at home. No matter what, the problems eventually cascade into the workplace. The length of time this takes depends upon the substance(s) and the particular employee. Yet inevitably the physical and emotional effects of dependency spill over, creating a variety of disciplinary problems and issues for managers.

In this chapter we examine the two primary forms of substance abuse: misuse of alcohol, and the use or possession of illegal and legal drugs. We discuss several forms of each abuse and consider what actions a firm might take in these different situations. Finally, we discuss the question of re-habilitation versus discipline and consider the use of Employee Assistance Programs (EAPs) and an employer's obligation to offer rehabilitation services as a reasonable accommodation.

OVERVIEW OF THE PROBLEM

Despite extensive efforts to educate the public on the risks of substance abuse, as well as serious governmental and organizational programs aimed at prosecuting and punishing offenders, alcohol and drug abuse continues to be a persistent, seemingly unsolvable problem. With estimates indicating that 10 to 20 percent of the general population is using illegal drugs, it is not surprising to find similar levels of drug use among the work force. In a recent Gallup poll, 22 percent of the 1,007 workers surveyed said that illegal drug use is "somewhat widespread" where they work. Forty-one percent believe that coworkers' drug use seriously affects their ability to do their own jobs. Eight percent had been offered drugs at work, and 7 percent had been approached to purchase drugs at work.[2] A Federal Railroad Administration study of 176 major collisions that took place in 1987 found that 65 percent of the fatalities involved drugs and/or alcohol.[3]

Although figures vary, it is conservatively estimated by government statisticians that at least 10 percent of all "problem employees" are alcoholics and that a large percentage of the grievances filed in many firms are alcohol-related. In the United States alone, alcohol abusers cost employers as much as $30 billion annually in lost production and may account for 40 percent or more of all industrial fatalities.[4] At least in the early stages, alcoholism may not lead to more on-the-job accidents, apparently because the person becomes more cautious. However, as the illness progresses, accident rates often increase and even in the early stages, the off-the-job rate for alcoholics may be three to four times greater than it would be for nonalcoholics.[5]

The eventual effects of alcoholism and drug abuse on the worker's health and work performance can be severe. At some point in the progression of this impairment, both the quality and quantity of work decline sharply and absenteeism increases, especially on Mondays, after holidays, and after paydays. In addition, mental on-the-job absenteeism often occurs as work performance declines. This in turn leads to morale problems among other employees, who now have to cover or correct the work of their impaired peers.

Obviously, the problem is too widespread and costly to ignore. How should an organization respond? Should it offer rehabilitation? If so, for what offenses? When does immediate discharge become the appropriate response? What is the best way to identify those who are impaired?

Should the firm conduct drug and alcohol testing? If it does, what are the legal issues involved?

ALCOHOLISM AS A DISCIPLINARY ISSUE

As the statistics clearly show, abuse of alcohol causes alarming economic loss and personal tragedy; and employees in all categories—from the shop to the executive suite—have proven to be susceptible. Several views regarding the etiology of alcoholism continue to be debated in the literature.[6] One perspective argues that it is a true physical disorder, whereas others contend that the problem is essentially the result of psychological problems. Proponents of the former position argue that people who become alcoholics are born with a specific physical vulnerability to the physiological effects of alcohol. As a result, their reaction to alcohol is more intense and they develop an overpowering need for the substance. The latter view suggests that people become alcoholics because in childhood they went through an array of disturbing emotional experiences that resulted in feelings of depression, repressed anger, and lowered self-esteem in later life. They use alcohol to build their damaged egos in order to "fit in" socially and relieve this long-standing emotional distress.

Others do not believe that alcoholism is an illness. To these people, alcoholics are weak-willed and lacking in self-discipline. The disease concept, they argue, implies that one is the helpless victim of biological or psychological determinism and is therefore powerless to truly correct the behavior. The best that can be hoped for is that with proper therapy, the condition can be controlled. The result of this, say the critics, is an unnecessary and unwise erosion of personal responsibility.[7]

In the field of labor arbitration, these various views become manifest in terms of three primary approaches. The first involves straightforward application of the traditional corrective model. Under this approach, employees are judged solely on the basis of job performance without reference to a clinical explanation for their shortcomings. Discharges are upheld as long as the employer has adhered to the provisions of the collective bargaining agreement with regard to work rules and use of the progressive penalty system. A second approach rejects corrective discipline in favor of a therapeutic model. In other words, the alcoholic employee is deemed to be the victim of a disorder and is offered opportunities to recover, including leaves of absence and appropriate treatment. The third approach operates on the theory that the employee suffers from an illness but ultimately may be subject to discharge, perhaps after being given one "second chance." This approach allows for a recovery opportunity while insisting that employees remain accountable for their behavior.[8]

Given these various points of view, it is not surprising that organizations differ considerably in how they deal with alcohol abuse. Some work with the employee to overcome the problem by means of counseling and re-habilitation programs. Others consider alcohol abuse a strictly disciplinary issue and take action based on either substandard performance or viola-tion of company rules. Still others use a combination of these two ap-proaches. In the following section we discuss several problem situations that managers face and suggest solutions to each.

The Employee Is Rumored to Be Drinking

Suppose a manager hears a rumor that an employee is drinking on the job or in near proximity to the workplace. Maybe it occurs during work or lunch breaks, or maybe the person is suspected of imbibing in a bar or restaurant off site. What action would be appropriate?

Assuming that the person's activities are not readily observable and they represent no safety risk to the person or others, the initial reaction may be to ignore the behavior. The problem is that although the manager may suspect that a rule violation has occurred, there is insufficient proof. Re-member, in disciplinary situations the employee is considered innocent until proven guilty and the burden of proof rests with the manager. The basic rule is that no action can be taken based solely on rumor or suspi-cion. What, then, should the manager do? One recommendation is to in-vestigate any accusations to see if they are supported by facts. Various employees could be interviewed, maybe by an outside party to insure im-partiality and to filter out personal bias. Keep in mind, however, that even though most people are honest, circumstances may cause them to withhold or distort information. In addition, other employees may not know the full truth; even if they do, some will be reluctant to come forward. They may fear reprisal or they may not want to say anything that can cause harm unless the situation is very serious.

When an employee seems almost too eager to volunteer damaging in-formation about someone, red flags should go up. Always consider the person's motives before acting, and try to find others who will corroborate the accusations.

How much proof does one need? There is no easy answer to this ques-tion. Some arbitrators have suggested that the severity and nature of the offense are important considerations. In other words, where was the em-ployee observed drinking; what type of alcoholic substance (e.g., beer as opposed to hard liquor) was being consumed; was the drinking at the beginning, during, or at the end of the workday? Because every offense and situation is unique, the approach taken by a manager must to some extent be custom-designed. Essentially, though, the amount and type of proof must be directly proportional to the proposed penalty.

Assuming that there is sufficient proof, the next step would be to decide on an appropriate correct action. In larger organizations, the prescribed course of action is probably spelled out in the employee handbook, union contract, or some other document. Small organizations may not have such documents, and managers have considerable leeway in determining the appropriate penalty or action. As a rule, the manager should select a response that is just sufficient to change the employee's behavior or eradicate the problem. In some cases a verbal warning may suffice; in other cases employees may have to be dismissed or sent to counseling.

The Employee Is under the Influence while at Work

It's one thing to hear rumors that an employee is taking an occasional drink or is an alcoholic, but what if the person appears intoxicated while on the job? The first step at this point is to determine whether the employee has a drinking problem. As Exhibit 6.1 shows, there are a number of typical tell-tale signs. These include altercations with other employees, unusual on-the-job accidents, poor judgment and bad decisions, and deteriorating personal appearance.[9]

In addition to looking for these indicators, some firms want managers to gather further proof by asking employees to take blood tests. This assumes that (1) the firm has procedures for doing so and a rule that specifies what degree of impairment or blood alcohol content (BAC) constitutes "under the influence," and (2) the rule is widely published.[10] If no specific BAC is set, most arbitrators apply the standard embodied in the state motor vehicle code.[11]

Exhibit 6.1
Symptoms of Alcohol Problems

---

1. Excessive absenteeism patterns: Monday, Friday and days before and after holidays.
2. Unexcused and frequent absences.
3. Tardiness and early departures.
4. Altercations with fellow employees.
5. Causing other employees injuries through negligence.
6. Poor judgment and bad decisions.
7. Unusual on-the-job accidents.
8. Increased spoilage and breakage of equipment through negligence.
9. Involvement with the law, such as wage attachments.
10. A deteriorating personal appearance.

The need for the BAC standard is reduced, however, if the firm also has a rule prohibiting employees from drinking within a certain number of hours before reporting to work. Rules specifying a period of eight hours are common, particularly in the transportation industry. The risk is that such rules can create the impression that by refraining from alcohol within the forbidden period, the employee may report to work confident that he/she is not "under the influence." Unfortunately, this is not always the case and an individual's elevated blood alcohol level may lead to disciplinary actions. Besides, preduty drinking bans present significant enforcement problems. It may be simpler to substitute for the hourly rule a requirement that the employee report to work with his/her faculties unimpaired, and that if behaviors warrant reasonable suspicion, an appropriate medical test will be administered.[12]

The real problem with the BAC standard is that its use requires that employees submit to invasive medical tests, a controversial requirement. For example, it has been argued that requiring an employee to submit to blood, breath, or urine tests constitutes a gross invasion of one's right to privacy. This argument has found some support in arbitral opinions; and recently, federal courts in Pennsylvania (*Borse v. Piece Goods Inc.*) and West Virginia (*Twiggy v. Hercules Corp.*)[13] have ruled that repeated random tests and testing procedures that are "highly offensive" violate public policy and may be viable cause for a wrongful discharge action. In addition, various arbitrators have held that an organization must seek the consent of the employee before the test is performed.[14]

A second concern is whether an employee can be discharged for refusing to submit to a test. Consider the case of a truck driver who was discharged for refusing to take a blood test following a minor accident at a loading dock. The collective bargaining agreement prohibited working while under the influence and authorized the employer to require a sobriety test. The contract even went so far as to state that an employee's refusal would be "prima facie evidence of being under the influence." The arbitrator ruled, however, that this one incident was not enough to indicate a drinking problem, so the employee was reinstated.[15]

A third issue involves the interpretation of the tests. Generally, the BAC tests are expressed as a percentage, whether the method is a drawn blood sample or breath or urine analysis. A result of 0.10 means that the alcohol constitutes one-tenth of the percent of the blood serum in the sample. However, although the BAC scale is widely used, there is no universally agreed upon point at which a person may be deemed substantially impaired by alcohol. Thus, it has become a common practice for companies to adopt the BAC standard used in the motor vehicle code of the state in which the employer is located.[16] Nevertheless, it is not a precise indicator of impairment for any given employee.

In summary, we argue that dealing with an employee who appears intoxicated while on the job is never a simple issue. Medical tests may be used to confirm one's suspicions, but, as the literature points out, they too can lead to problems. Therefore, as a general rule a prudent manager should have other evidence (such as those shown in Exhibit 6.1) before taking severe disciplinary actions.

The Employee's Performance Is Deteriorating

Sometimes an employee seems to be slipping in terms of performance and the manager is not sure why. Alcohol might be the problem, but there are other causes to consider. The safe approach is for the manager to focus strictly on the declining performance and to follow the requirements of the company disciplinary policy. If the employee has frequent absenteeism, tardiness, erratic work, accidents, or general moodiness and belligerence, the best advice is to focus on these problems and avoid making accusations regarding the employee's drinking. In so doing, a manager can offer the employee psychological support and encourage him/her to face up to the underlying problem, whatever it is.

Testing employees whose performance is deteriorating is not usually appropriate because the manager does not have "reasonable suspicion." Of course, the manager could try to gather further evidence if an alcohol problem is suspected. In the meantime the manager should focus on the employee's work performance and implement the progressive penalty system and/or corrective counseling procedures if needed.[17]

DRUG ABUSE AS A DISCIPLINARY ISSUE

Although alcoholism as a treatable disorder is an idea that has gained ground in recent years, there is still considerable opposition to rehabilitating employees who are dependent upon illegal drugs. There are several reasons for this resistance. First, alcoholism is a much more familiar disorder than other forms of chemical abuse. Second, drugs such as marijuana have been primarily associated with younger members of the work force, whereas management, union leaders, and arbitrators are usually more senior and generally not sympathetic to drug use or users. Third, because drug involvement is often a criminal offense, managers tend to characterize the problem more in terms of law enforcement than in terms of therapy.

Even though drug use by an employee can be illegal, one should not forget that employees also abuse a variety of lawfully obtained prescription drugs or over-the-counter drugs. Legitimate medications are frequently misused: too much is taken too often, or they are combined with alcohol. This is particularly true of tranquilizers like Valium, antidepressants like Prozac, and a number of other psychoactive prescription drugs.

Employees may also be abusing a substance that is not technically a drug or medicine, as in the case of glue sniffing. Nevertheless, the primary concern in most organizations is what to do when employees are using a so-called street drug such as cocaine, marijuana, or heroin.[18] As with alcohol, there are several situations that managers face.

The Employee Is Selling Drugs at Work

Selling or distributing drugs at work generally affords clear grounds for immediate dismissal. Employers argue that such a penalty is warranted by the severity of the offense. Even if there are no contractual provisions or company rules explicitly prohibiting drugs or if summary discharge conflicts with the contractual requirements for progressive discipline, most arbitrators would argue that a firm can still terminate employees on the basis of one occurrence because of the severity of the offense; the sale of drugs usually does not warrant a second chance.[19]

The only real concern involves the question of proof and how evidence was obtained. An isolated or anonymous report may not be sufficient, because accusing someone without proper evidence could lead to a later charge of defamation and/or wrongful discharge. In this case the employer may want to conduct a search of the premises in an effort to confirm the allegations.

In addition, there may be questions regarding the methods used to obtain the evidence. However, the constitutional protection against unreasonable search and seizure only applies to the actions of government against citizens; it does not limit an organization's ability to search employees' lockers or desks. Yet many employees presume they have a right to privacy, and in some situations this may lead to legal actions. To be safe, therefore, managers should make it clear to employees that all company property including business equipment, computers, desks, and lockers belong to the employer and may be subject to search or investigation without prior notice.

Although arbitrators are typically not sympathetic to employees charged with the sale or distribution of drugs while at work, a number of them are reluctant to sustain severe disciplinary actions when the alleged incidents have occurred while individuals are off duty. However, even in these situations severe penalties have been upheld when the employer was able to demonstrate that the off-duty conduct adversely affected its business or reputation, threatened the welfare or morale of other employees, or rendered the grievant unfit to perform his/her duties.[20] When any of these conditions exist and the charges can be substantiated beyond a reasonable doubt, the firm's actions are justified.

The Employee Possesses Drugs

A second situation that might arise is an individual found to be possessing drugs while at work but apparently not selling or distributing them to other employees. Although in this scenario there are issues related to the type of drug and the amount of the substance, it is generally believed that because possession of drugs is a criminal offense the person should be summarily dismissed. Besides, possession could easily lead to sale and distribution. The one valid defense that an employee might offer is that the drugs were planted by someone else. Clearly, this is something to consider before taking action, especially when a manager inadvertently stumbles upon the substance while looking for something else in a person's desk or locker.

Suppose, however, that the person does not have the drugs at work, but at home. Consider the case of a refinery employee who was arrested and charged with possession of drugs with an intent to sell. In this situation the materials (one pound of cocaine and two pounds of marijuana) were found in his home. The union argued that because the grievant had not possessed or sold drugs at work, his punishment should be solely that which the criminal justice system meted out rather than an employment penalty. In this case, even though the offense occurred off duty, the discharge was upheld because the arbitrator discerned a nexus to the job in that it raised the possibility that the drug trafficking was not confined to off-duty hours.[21]

But what if the drugs are off site and the firm has no policy or there is no nexus to the job? This was the situation in the arbitration case of a warehouse worker who was discharged after pleading guilty to a cocaine possession charge following police discovery of 116.5 grams of cocaine in his house. Although the company regarded the employee as "a major drug dealer," the arbitrator observed that the firm lacked a rule against illegal possession of drugs at home and the possible effects of bad publicity did not link the criminal offense to his job. The arbitrator reinstated the employee with full back pay.[22]

Working under the Influence of Drugs

The last situation involves employees who are working while under the influence of drugs. Even though this is normally considered a very serious offense justifying immediate dismissal, to avoid claims of discrimination and wrongful discharge the firm may want to confirm its suspicions by requiring the person to take a drug test. At the same time, any employee who is suspected of current drug use and has a job in which safety is a consideration should be immediately transferred to other duties until test results can be obtained.

If the organization is a federal contractor, the law requires an ongoing effort to identify drug problems. According to the Drug-Free Workplace Act of 1988, any contractor who does as little as $15,000 worth of business with any federal entity must provide assurances of a drug-free workplace. Nevertheless, caution is advised because federal and state laws sometimes collide or overlap. For example, in some states there are limitations on the types of programs a firm can initiate. Moreover, National Labor Relations Board precedent requires that programs first be negotiated with the appropriate unions.

When it appears that a number of employees are working while under the influence, an organization-wide testing program may be the best approach. But before such a program is initiated, the firm must decide what the program will seek to accomplish; and even though traditional drug testing may ultimately emerge as the best alternative, there are other choices to consider.[23]

Employers who desire an objective measure of fitness or impairment have the option of performance or fitness testing that can be closely tailored to the job. Unlike drug testing, these options seem to enjoy widespread support. For example, pilots can be tested on flight simulators and given similar tests that measure driving skills, coordination, balance, and reflexes in realistic work settings. Other jobs may have similar tests. Unlike traditional drug testing, performance/fitness testing can be readily incorporated into the work routine, measures current impairment, requires no bodily fluid samples, and does not intrude on an employee's life off the job. Another advantage is that such tests register impairments from any source, not just drugs; they therefore provide a much more inclusive safety check.

Once the firm has decided that testing of bodily fluids should be done, it must establish the "rules of the road" and spell them out to all employees. Unfortunately, despite widespread use of traditional drug-testing programs in the private sector, at present there is no universally accepted or court-approved procedural model or guide. However, industry experts, business groups, and federal agencies do concur on a few guidelines, many of which can be found in the *Mandatory Guidelines* developed by the National Institute on Drug Abuse (NIDA) for federal workplace drug testing.[24]

Paramount among these guidelines is that test results must always be unquestionably reliable and defensible in a legal proceeding or arbitration hearing. Even a single false positive is unacceptable. The good news is that testing methodology has evolved to the point that if it is properly performed and confirmed, it is considered extremely reliable and valid. According to NIDA, although it is theoretically possible for a substance other than the drug in question to give a positive result, false positives are usually the result of human error. How, then, does one ensure accuracy?

Use a NIDA-certified laboratory whenever possible. Such a lab has met strict NIDA standards, including initial certification that requires three successive rounds of performance testing in which the lab must determine accurately the type and concentration of the drug in twenty prepared specimens. A single false positive disqualifies the lab from further consideration. Maintenance of certification requires participation in bimonthly performance testing as well as biannual on-site inspections. Currently, approximately 80 of the estimated 1,200 drug-testing labs in the United States are NIDA-certified.

If a NIDA-certified facility is not available, the firm should at least determine whether the staff in the lab it is using has been certified by the state. These requirements vary from state to state, so it is best to inquire. The lab should also have its own internal certification and training program for every technical position and for each procedure performed.[25]

In addition, the lab should be using strict quality control procedures and should be making an ongoing effort to maintain the chain of custody for specimens being tested. To ensure the chain of custody, a set of forms, labels, and documents must follow each specimen and be signed, dated, and noted by each individual who comes into contact with it.[26]

A second important guideline is that a company should always strive to ensure that the testing program respects one's personal dignity. For example, even though most testing programs that use urine specimens require that persons be monitored while giving the sample, there are limits. In a recent arbitration decision, humiliation due to micturition monitoring was held to be a legitimate reason for refusing a test. In this case a female employee wearing a leotard would have had to undress completely in front of a stranger (a female nurse) to provide the urine sample. She requested a robe, but this was denied. The arbitrator agreed that her request was reasonable and that firing her for refusal to submit did not constitute just cause for her discharge. The grievant was reinstated with back pay.[27]

A third guideline is that employees be treated fairly and be informed of the "rules." For example, NIDA[28] recommends that:

- When managers have reasonable cause to suspect drug use, they should gather all information and facts supporting their suspicions. They should seek higher level concurrence and prepare a written report detailing the basis for suspicion. Only then should the employee be notified.

- Employees should be notified in advance if the firm intends to test persons involved in on-the-job accidents. The criteria for such an accident or unsafe practice testing should be clearly stated.

- If the firm intends to use random testing, it has an obligation to alert employees that they are subject to random testing and have them sign an acknowledgment form. In addition, minimal notice (two hours is recommended) should be provided before the test is conducted.

• In all cases, the notification of possible or mandatory drug testing should give employees the chance to voluntarily admit to a problem and be referred to treatment before dismissal.

Finally, confidentiality guidelines tend to be clear-cut. Drug test results are confidential medical information and must be kept separate from other employee records. Results may not be disclosed without the employee's consent; and an individual may, upon written request, have access to his/her own drug test records.[29]

REHABILITATING SUBSTANCE ABUSERS

Many organizations now believe that alcohol and drug abusers are owed a second chance and that it is in the firm's best interest to provide offenders with an opportunity to become rehabilitated. The Americans with Disabilities Act does require that companies hire handicapped persons, and in some cases substance abusers (mainly alcohol abusers) are so defined. Generally, this requires some effort at rehabilitation to insure that the person can do the job and not be a risk to others.[30]

Although some firms such as Exxon Corporation have declared that even after treatment known substance abusers won't be returned to so-called critical jobs, many other large employers attempt to rehabilitate before dismissal. In most cases this involves the establishment of an Employee Assistance Program (EAP) run by the employer, a union, or a joint effort.[31]

The history of EAPs is closely intertwined with alcohol abuse treatment and Alcoholics Anonymous. In fact, the first EAPs were occupational alcohol programs started by larger companies in the 1940s. The modern EAP was born in the early 1960s, when the concept was expanded to provide treatment for other problems such as marital discord, family trouble, and financial difficulties. The program at DuPont de Nemours is a good example of this evolution.[32]

In 1942 Maurice DuPont Lee, a member of senior management at DuPont, met Bill Wilson, the cofounder of a newly organized self-help group called Alcoholics Anonymous (AA). From that meeting sprang an interest in helping DuPont employees who were abusing alcohol; and in 1944 the company formally established one of the first occupational alcoholism programs in the country.

Early in the DuPont program, AA was the only treatment resource; but when other programs became established during the 1960s, DuPont was quick to include the costs of such treatment in its employee benefits package. The program initially dealt with alcoholism counseling and treatment, but in the late 1970s it branched out to include drug addiction as well.

As with most organizations, the EAP at DuPont can be activated in several ways: an employee voluntarily seeks help; a supervisor refers the employee; the spouse of a troubled employee seeks the program's help. Once a person is in the program, EAP consultants help in diagnosing problems and direct employees to treatment programs within the community. If that involves a residential or in-patient facility, the company health coverage pays 80 percent of the costs.

Although there is no formal evaluation of the EAP at DuPont, the feedback from management and employees indicates that it is a success. Employees' expectations companywide are expressed in the statement that "If I have a substance abuse problem, I can get help." But as the program director points out, the company does not ask that the program justify its existence in terms of cost effectiveness, rehabilitation success rates, employee usage rates, or other indicators.

For those involved with arbitration, the most salient question posed by the EAP movement is whether the employer—who maintains or recognizes an EAP or even promulgates a policy on substance abuse—incurs an obligation to try rehabilitation before discharge. As we noted earlier, firms have generally been more willing to offer rehabilitation for alcoholism than for drug abuse, and arbitrators have been wary of overturning discharges for drug use on the grounds that the employee should have been offered a chance for rehabilitation. However, some arbitrators have drawn the line at discharging an employee while he/she is actively involved in a drug treatment program.

In one case an employer discharged a mill janitor when it was discovered that he was on a methadone treatment program. The company maintained that methadone, like heroin, is an addictive narcotic that impairs the user's reactions and judgment. After reviewing the case the arbitrator rejected this contention and ordered the man to be reinstated.[33]

When safety is not an overriding consideration, legal experts argue that the company should at least give a second chance to an employee who seems to be recovering but suffers a relapse. Two chances should also suffice to satisfy government standards of reasonable accommodation. Three chances that are preceded by counseling and progressive discipline should by any standard satisfy the firm's obligation to substance abusers. Nevertheless, as the case of *Rodgers v. Lehman* points out, the situation is never simple.[34]

In this situation Rodgers, a Department of the Navy employee, never drank on the job. Nor did he ever report to work drunk. His alcoholism was characterized by binge drinking—excessive drinking followed by abstinence—and blackouts. In 1978 and 1979 he was absent nearly fifty days each year. He was placed on controlled leave and warned of potential disciplinary action. In 1980 and 1981 the absences continued. In 1982 his physicians indicated for the first time that he was suffering from alcoholism.

Rodgers was then counseled and advised that if he did not accept treatment, he would be progressively disciplined. He was referred to, but refused to attend, counseling. His absences continued throughout 1982, and he was again warned of potential disciplinary action and given an unsatisfactory performance rating. He then entered a hospital's detoxification unit for nine days. Upon his return to work, he attended Alcoholics Anonymous (AA) meetings. His work attendance record improved, but six months later he stopped attending the AA meetings. Due to alcohol abuse, his attendance record again deteriorated. After missing several days at work and calling in one day to say he was "drunk as a skunk," he was advised to obtain counseling. Rodgers again refused. He was then warned to attend counseling sessions or risk losing his job. He took that warning to heart, attended AA meetings, and for the next three months incurred no absences.

Rodgers's alcohol-related absences then resumed. He was warned that his absences were unacceptable and that disciplinary action would result. Rodgers then successfully completed outpatient counseling, attended AA meetings, and for five months had improved attendance. He then relapsed, began drinking again, missed work, and was given a fourteen-day suspension for absences. Upon his return his absences continued, and he was counseled that he risked discharge. Rodgers then entered an inpatient rehabilitation center. After a month's attendance, his counselor wrote that Rodgers "made a connection and identification with his disease," that he had "begun to deal with issues of life," and that his "prognosis is good." Nonetheless, within a month of his return to work Rodgers was discharged because he had been "offered assistance for [his] medical problem a number of times, but had failed to correct [his] unreliable and undependable conduct."

Although noting the "extreme tolerance and patience" exhibited by the agency, the court also noted that Rodgers was deprived of an opportunity to participate in an inpatient treatment program before being discharged. The failure to do so breached the employer's duty to accommodate and warranted a judgment, including reinstatement, in Rodgers's favor.

In its ruling on *Rodgers*, the court recognized five steps that should be taken when an employee's poor job performance is suspected to result from alcoholism:

1. The employee should be informed of available counseling services.

2. If the employee's unsatisfactory job performance continues, the employee should be given a "firm choice" between treatment and discipline. The employee should be clearly and unequivocally warned that unsatisfactory job performance caused by drinking will eventually result in discipline, including the termination of employment.

3. Unless it is clear in a particular case that inpatient treatment is immediately

required, the employee should be permitted to participate initially in outpatient treatment of sufficient duration to ensure him a reasonable opportunity for cure. If the employee continues to drink while participating in that treatment, progressive discipline may be imposed for any resulting job-related misconduct.

4. If the employee ceases to participate in the outpatient treatment, is discharged for noncooperation or continues to drink after completion of that treatment, and is guilty of job-related misconduct, the employer should afford the employee an opportunity to participate in an inpatient program before discharging him/her. This program should be paid for with accrued or unpaid leave, unless the employer can establish it would suffer an undue hardship from the employee's absence.

5. If the employee completes the program but thereafter relapses and then fails to perform his/her job satisfactorily, a decision to discharge him/her will be presumed to be reasonable. Only in a rare case, such as when a recovering alcoholic has had a single relapse after a prolonged period of abstinence, can this presumption be rebutted.

CONCLUSION

Historically, managers have paid little attention to the issue of substance abuse. In recent years, however, it has become a major concern due largely to the fact that drug and alcohol abuse has become increasingly prevalent within the work force. Most organizations approach the problem in one of three ways. Some work with the afflicted employee to overcome the problem through counseling and rehabilitation. A number of large firms have even set up extensive treatment centers. Others consider substance abuse a disciplinary problem and sanction employees for failure to perform on the job or for violating the firm's drug/alcohol rules. The third alternative is to use a combination approach.

Even though alcohol and drugs are part of the same problem (in fact, employees often abuse both), we have chosen to discuss them separately in this chapter. Clearly, however, there is significant overlap. The real difference is in terms of our perceptions of alcohol versus drug abuses. The alcohol-abusing employee is much more likely to be treated with tolerance and offered rehabilitation options than is the employee who abuses other drugs.

No matter how the firm approaches substance abuse, there are various conditions and situations to consider. The substance may be used on the job or off the job. The employee may or may not be under the influence while at work. The person may be distributing to others. Maybe the manager doesn't worry about any of these but chooses to focus on deteriorating work performance.

A variety of legal concerns—such as having sufficient proof, respecting privacy, and using methods of detection that are not overly invasive—must be considered carefully. The firm must decide whether or not to test; if so, should it be company-wide or random? In either case, employees should at least know the ground rules and be aware of situations that might lead to tests being performed.

The bottom line is that substance abuse is a pervasive, extremely complex problem that does not lend itself to simple solutions. An effective manager must recognize that (1) given the statistics, some employees are likely to be afflicted, and (2) a clear, rational response is necessary. Regardless of which strategy or strategies are selected by an organization, a carefully conceived program for addressing substance abuse is a must.

NOTES

1. E. J. Miller, "Investing in a Drug-Free Workplace," *HR Magazine*, May 1991.

2. Bureau of National Affairs, Inc. "Workers Support Drug Testing," *Bulletin to Management*, January 4, 1990.

3. J. Shear, "Risk of Wrecks Puts Heat on Railways' Federal Overseer," *Insight*, May 9, 1988.

4. G. Pate and J. Adkins, Jr., "The Employer's Role in Alcoholism Assistance," *Personnel Journal*, July 1983.

5. H. Trice, "Alcoholism and the Work World," *Sloan Management Review*, Fall 1970.

6. T. S. Denenberg and R. V. Denenberg, *Alcohol and Other Drugs* (Washington, DC: Bureau of National Affairs, 1991).

7. Ibid.

8. Ibid.

9. S. H. Applebaum, "Diagnosing and Counseling the Alcoholic Employee for Mutual Benefit," *Personnel Administrator*, August 1982.

10. Denenberg and Denenberg, *Alcohol and Other Drugs*.

11. Ibid.

12. Ibid.

13. Ibid.

14. Ibid.

15. Ibid.

16. Ibid.

17. J. A. Segal, "To Test or Not to Test," *HR Magazine*, April 1992.

18. Denenberg and Denenberg, *Alcohol and Other Drugs*.

19. Ibid. See also J. R. Redeker, *Employee Discipline: Policies and Practices* (Washington, DC: Bureau of National Affairs, 1989).

20. Denenberg and Denenberg, *Alcohol and Other Drugs*.

21. Ibid.

22. Ibid.

23. R. L. James, "Should You Have a Drug Testing Program?" *Foundry*, April 1992.

24. R. Brookler, "Industry Standards in Workplace Drug Testing," *Personnel Journal*, April 1982.

25. Ibid.

26. Ibid.

27. Ibid.

28. Ibid.

29. M. Denis, "Alcoholics and Drug Abusers—How Many Second Chances Are They Owed?" *Employment Relations Today*, Autumn 1989.

30. "Firms Debate Hard Line on Alcoholics," *Wall Street Journal*, April 13, 1989.

31. D. W. Myers, *Employee Assistance Programs: Drug, Alcohol and Other Problems* (Washington, D.C.: Commerce Clearing House, 1986).

32. Denenberg and Denenberg, *Alcohol and Other Drugs*.

33. Denis, "Alcoholics and Drug Abusers."

34. Ibid.

Chapter 7

Controlling Employee Absenteeism

Rick Stone, an Air Force sergeant, is a shift supervisor in the control tower, primarily issuing takeoff and landing instructions to incoming and departing aircraft. Rick is also a top-notch golfer, nearly as good as some professionals. In fact, a year ago he won the Air Force–wide golf tournament. Whenever dignitaries visit the base, Rick is invited to join the golf outing. He is, of course, excused from work on these occasions.

Unfortunately, Captain White, the commanding officer in charge of the air traffic controllers, has found Rick's outside activities to be a major nuisance. Because of budget cuts, he is very short of qualified controllers and needs every one he has. He assigns Rick for duty but never knows if Rick will be there.

Rick frequently seems to have a legitimate excuse for missing work, often an excused-from-duty slip from a base doctor or dentist for a variety of suspicious ailments. Once, as an example, there was a big golf match at another base. Rick just so happened to have a problem with his leg, so he was sent to that base hospital for observation. The attending physician who authorized this happened to be a golfing buddy of his. Rick played in the match after his leg healed almost miraculously. At other times, Rick would be excused from work because he was on the base or squadron golf team.

Captain White is wondering what he can do without upsetting Rick or the brass. Rick is certainly a good controller, but he just can't be depended upon to show up. Other senior controllers have to cover for him repeatedly, thus creating a hardship on them and causing hard feelings toward Rick. How can Captain White address this problem without making matters worse and jeopardizing his own career?

Absenteeism is a problem in most organizations. As this case suggests, when people are absent it creates problems both for the supervisor and for the coworkers who have to cover for them. In this chapter we discuss various approaches a manager might use to deal with absenteeism and we point out what actions a manager needs to take or avoid when facing this problem.

THE NATURE OF THE PROBLEM

Employee absenteeism is an issue that affects organizations in a variety of ways. How much of a problem is it? According to one broad-based survey conducted by the Bureau of National Affairs, in 1992 unscheduled absenteeism amounted to 1.6 percent of scheduled workdays.[1] Larger firms had higher rates of absenteeism than smaller firms (1.9% vs. 1.4%). This translates into an average employee missing approximately four days of work a year that are unanticipated and unscheduled. These absences are estimated to cost between $26 billion and $46 billion nationally[2]; if one adds the costs associated with other leaves such as vacations, jury duty, military leave, funeral leave, and paid holidays, the dollar figures are even higher. Furthermore, one could add the costs associated with coffee breaks, lunch breaks, and socializing with others.

From the point of view of an individual firm, absenteeism can create substantial costs. If, for example, an individual is absent due to illness, the firm may be liable for a day's pay under the sick leave policy. In addition, overtime may need to be paid to cover for the absent employee. In some cases temporary help may have to be hired and supervisors must spend time finding a replacement or may have to fill in themselves. Furthermore, other employees may have to work harder, which may lead to greater stress, reduced morale, and hard feelings toward the absent worker. In some cases, work simply doesn't got done at all or is delayed until the employee returns. This can lead to lost sales, poor customer service, more accidents, communication breakdowns, and disruptions to the work flow. In some cases these represent the largest costs of all.

How much does absenteeism cost your firm? We suggest that it's more than you might think. According to a recent Commerce Clearing House study,[3] the cost of paid sick leave alone ranges on average from $200 per person per year for firms with less than 250 employees to $620 for firms with 250–499 employees. The cost for firms with 500 or more employees averages between $500 and $569, depending on the firm's size. These figures were calculated by dividing the total dollars spent on paid sick leave by the number of employees and excluding all other indirect costs. A study at St. Luke's Hospital in Milwaukee, Wisconsin, showed 182,700 hours of absenteeism. At the average hourly wage of $6.50, the hospital had lost time costs of $1,187,550 in a single year. A survey of hospital managers revealed that more than half of this absenteeism was not for genuine sickness. Rather, it represented vacation extensions, mental health days, illnesses in the family, and other personal time off. Thus, sick leave abuse was estimated to cost the firm $593,775 annually.[4]

Clearly, firms must consider absenteeism as a cost center just as they do equipment, training programs, supplies, and other factors.[5] They must manage it by tracking and documenting the costs (at least the amount paid to individuals for time not worked) and try to minimize the expense, because firms that incur lower absenteeism costs do have a competitive advantage.

Even though absenteeism costs are high, managers need to weigh them against the potential benefits. For example, what if sick workers come to work even if they are really sick and spread the illness to others? In addition, the sick worker may not perform well and make costly errors or get into accidents. Even one poor decision may be far more expensive than the cost of paying for the employee's sick leave. Furthermore, by working instead of staying home to recover, the employee may aggravate the illness and end up needing expensive hospitalization or an extended leave.

In some firms employees are not paid for days missed due to illness. Therefore, having an employee miss work may be beneficial, particularly if the work load is low. Indeed, some firms may even encourage absenteeism under these conditions. In some cases absenteeism may actually help morale and group effectiveness by removing, at least temporarily, an employee who is disliked and actually interferes with teamwork.

Another often unrecognized benefit is that absenteeism may result in workers acquiring an increased knowledge of others' jobs. When someone covers for an absent colleague, they may learn the job and have a greater understanding of the problems associated with it. The hidden long-term benefit in this situation is greater work scheduling flexibility, a better-trained work force, and perhaps greater coordination among employees. It may also reduce job monotony and enhance the employee's promotion potential.

However, absenteeism is essentially a symptom of other problems faced on a daily basis by employees. As we noted in Chapter 3, everyone occasionally misses a day because of illness in the family, car problems, inclement weather, other commitments such as medical/dental appointments, and the like. The otherwise reliable employee who misses now and then is not the employee that this chapter addresses. We want to discuss the chronic offender and consider what a manager can do to make this person more reliable. Always remember that every individual is different, so managers need to know what is causing the problem and then be flexible in seeking solutions.

Also, keep in mind that the new Family and Medical Leave Act does require that firms with 50 or more employees within a 75-mile radius offer workers as much as 12 weeks of unpaid leave after childbirth or adoption;

to care for a seriously ill child, spouse, or parent; or in the case of an employee's own serious illness. Employers will have to continue health care coverage during the leave and must guarantee employees that they will return to either the same job or a comparable position. Employers may exempt "key employees," defined as the highest-paid 10 percent of the work force, whose leave would cause economic harm to the employer. A qualifying condition is seen as the need for continuing care and the inability to perform one's job or the need to care for an ill family member.

DEALING WITH ABSENTEEISM

Over the past few years, firms large and small have developed various strategies for dealing with absenteeism. Many organizations use highly punitive methods that rely primarily on strict enforcement of disciplinary procedures. Others take a more positive approach and reward employees for being at work. Still others use a combination approach involving both rewards for good attendance and punitive steps. A recent Commerce Clearing House (CCH) study asked almost 900 firms how they dealt with absenteeism. Firms were allowed to indicate more than one response: 668 stated that they used disciplinary action; 460 had a no-fault policy; 426 used a year-end review; 312 used personal recognition; 168 paid bonuses for good attendance; 182 had a buyback program for employees who did not use all their allotted sick leave; and 138 had a paid leave bank.[6]

The study also found that the perceived effectiveness of the various methods depended somewhat upon whether the employees were salaried or hourly workers. For hourly workers the order (from most to least effective) was paid leave bank, bonus, no-fault, discipline, buyback, yearly review, and recognition. For salaried the following order was reported: paid leave bank, discipline, bonus, recognition, no-fault, buyback, and yearly review. Keep in mind that these findings are based on manager perceptions, not a rigorous scientific comparison of the seven approaches. Nonetheless, the collective judgments of so many "experts" is hard to ignore.

Taking Disciplinary Action

As we have seen, a study by the Commerce Clearing House[7] found that disciplinary action is the most common program for controlling absenteeism. This involves developing an absenteeism policy; communicating it to all employees; and then taking disciplinary action toward offenders, following the firm's progressive penalty system.

Typical Policies

Disciplinary policies range in length from very short to extremely comprehensive. Elaborate policies typically cover the need to be at one's work station, a call-in procedure, illness at work, absence notification, physician letters, attendance records, and disciplinary penalties.

Being at one's work station. In writing policies, firms often stress the need to be at one's work site. For example, one shipyard states that employees are subject to discharge or other discipline for: (1) repeated tardiness or absence; (2) quitting work before the scheduled end of shift or exceeding specified time for lunch; (3) leaving the plant during scheduled working hours without proper authorization; and (4) leaving the work station during scheduled work periods without authorization from the supervisor except in the performance of duties.

Absence notification. Some firms' policies address the issue of calling in if one expects to be late or miss work. For example, one hotel states:

the smooth running of our Hotel depends on each employee reporting to work on time and as scheduled. If you are unable to report to work on time for any reason, you must notify your supervisor immediately. If you are unable to reach your supervisor, have him/her paged by the Hotel operator or leave a message with the Assistant Manager. It is your responsibility to inform your supervisor. Do not rely on friends, relatives, or fellow employees to inform your supervisor. Failure to inform your supervisor or the Assistant Manager on duty will result in disciplinary action. If a situation arises where you are unable to come to work at all, you must let your supervisor or the Assistant Manager on duty know of your absence at least two (2) hours in advance of your shift. If you do not call in at least two (2) hours in advance, you will not be eligible for sick pay.

Another organization has a similar policy:

Employee attendance is crucially important to the success of any business. In the hospitality industry it is particularly important due to the fact that all of our employees must be congenial and motivated at all times. This could be difficult to achieve if an employee's relief does not show up and that employee ends up working a double shift. If you do have to be absent from work, you should notify your supervisor as much in advance as possible, so we can try to find another employee to work your shift. Always remember, the resort is a 24 hour business and others (your peers) are relying on your commitment to be on time.

The policy adds that two unexcused absences (not calling in, not reporting to work) are grounds for immediate dismissal.

A common addition to many policies is a statement addressed to employees who miss work for several days without calling their boss. For example, one hotel's policy states, "Any employee who fails to report to work without notifying his/her supervisor for three consecutive days will constitute a 'Voluntary Quit' and be terminated from the Hotel's payroll." This policy protects the firm and allows it to replace the missing worker.

Physician's excuse. Many absenteeism policies include the requirement that the absent employee present a physician's letter when returning to work. This letter may describe the employee's illness, attest to the fact that the employee was ill, or state that the employee is sufficiently well to return to work. For example, one hotel chain states, "employees who are absent due to personal illness for 3 consecutive days may be required to provide a doctor's excuse."

Employee illness at work. The issue of what actions an employee is to take in the event of illness at work is covered in some policies. As an example, one retail store states the following policy:

If you become ill at work and feel you cannot continue to work, please contact your Manager or the Personnel Office. Associates who become ill at work, and are released to go home by their Manager and/or Personnel Office, will receive pay according to the following guidelines:

A. Full-time and part-time associates will be paid for actual hours worked with a minimum guarantee of three hours pay.

B. Flex associates will be paid for actual hours worked.

Attendance records. Attendance policies cover how employees are to keep track of hours worked. For example, one firm states:

You are responsible for maintaining a record of your hours worked through the completion of an attendance card or by registering an attendance card in a time clock. These cards are the record of the hours you worked and are used for computing pay. If an employee who is required to punch the time clock leaves the premises for lunch, he or she must punch out, and punch in on return to work. Each employee is responsible for punching his or her own time card. The punching of another's card is not permitted. Anyone violating this policy is subject to disciplinary action. Be sure to clock in at the start of the day and clock out at the end of the day.

Disciplinary penalties. The penalty associated with being absent without notification varies from firm to firm. Some take a rather legalistic approach and spell how exactly what the penalty will be, whereas others are less specific. To illustrate, one firm that uses a broad approach states without further explanation that excessive absenteeism will result in "disciplinary action." On the other hand, a large amusement park states:

Absenteeism is considered excessive if you have 4 or more unscheduled absences in a rolling 90-day period. Each tardiness counts as 1/2 of an absence. Therefore, 2 tardies will be counted as one absence in determining good attendance. Any combination of tardiness and absence that equals 4 or more will result in termination in employment.

Arbitrator Recommendations

In reviewing absenteeism cases, arbitrators follow a fairly systematic process. At the onset, they look at the reasonableness of the attendance rule and make sure it is consistent with the labor agreement. They then check to see if employees were made aware of the rule and whether the rule has been consistently enforced. They examine the case to determine if the employee had been told the probable consequences of continued absence and if the firm was following the progressive penalty system. Failure to meet these requirements may be a sufficient reason to lessen or void the penalty imposed.[8]

In determining the appropriate penalty, arbitrators recommend that managers examine the employee's work record, past disciplinary record, length of service, and the severity of the offense (e.g., the effect on efficiency and morale, the number of absences, the length of time during which the employee had a poor attendance record, the nature of the employee's job, the attendance records of other employees, and whether the absences were chronic or intermittent). They also suggest that mitigating circumstances be considered such as the reasons for the worker's absence and the likelihood of improved attendance.

The importance of this last point is reinforced by various published decisions. In one, an employee at Automotive Distributors was chronically absent due to a sinus condition but had not sought treatment in a year and a half. The firm discharged the employee. The arbitrator agreed and noted that the employee's attendance was not likely to improve given his failure to seek help.[9] In another case an employee at Champion International was discharged for absenteeism as well. The arbitrator refused to reinstate her because she admitted that her excessive absenteeism was due to her dislike of her job. He reasoned that the employee's attendance was not likely to improve.[10] On the other hand, an employee at Menasha Corporation had been absent due to an illness that doctors suspected was cancer. The arbitrator reversed the discharge because the employee had subsequently learned that he did not have cancer, and therefore he was likely to have better attendance.[11]

The issue of management's right to terminate for excessive absence has surfaced in a number of cases. In general, arbitrators have recognized a standard that gives employers the right to discipline, up to and including termination, for excessive absences, even if they are due to illness. For example, in an often-cited case, Arbitrator Teple stated:

At some point the employer must be able to terminate the services of an employee who is unable to work more than part time, for whatever reason. Efficiency and ability to compete can hardly be maintained if employees cannot be depended upon to work with reasonable regularity. Other arbitrators have so found, and this

Arbitrator has upheld terminations in several appropriate cases involving frequent and extended absences due to illness.[12]

These cases raise the question of what constitutes "excessive absenteeism." One arbitrator has stated that there is no set standard or magical number that can be used to determine when absences due to illness, or illness-related causes, become excessive. Rather, a number of factors are considered on a case-by-case basis. These include the number of absences specified in the union-management contract or in the company work rules, or the number applied in previous cases. Also considered are the length of time an employee has had a poor record of attendance, the reason for the absences (e.g., illness, transportation problem, family difficulties), and the timing of the absences (on which days they occurred).[13]

A common absenteeism problem occurs when one manager recognizes that the policy is flawed and that one or more employees have learned to "work the system." In response, the manager may try to correct the problem on an ad hoc basis and create special rules that apply only to a given employee. The problem in this situation is that the new rule may be inconsistent with the union-management agreement and may not be applied by all the other managers. If managers cannot accept the absenteeism level permitted by the system, then a new system must be negotiated and applied consistently.[14]

Research Results

The effectiveness of disciplinary systems in controlling absenteeism has been examined in so few studies that clear-cut conclusions are hard to draw. A review of the literature by two researchers revealed only seven studies that examined the use of discipline alone as a control method. Six of these reported that the particular aspect of discipline examined was effective in improving attendance.[15]

The recent CCH study found that almost 900 respondents rated it fourth most effective (behind paid leave bank, bonuses, and no-fault) for hourly workers and second most effective for salaried workers (paid leave bank was rated more effective).[16]

A field study conducted in a facility for the mentally retarded demonstrated the effectiveness of having employees call in to report their absence. The important finding here was that the critical factor was who the employee contacted and the nature of the contact. Absenteeism was lowest when the employee was required to call his/her immediate supervisor (not a central absence control person) and when the supervisor asked about the nature of the illness, whether the employee planned to see a doctor, the name of the doctor, and when the employee expected to return to work.[17]

The effect of requiring a written doctor's excuse was examined in a study at Southern Bell–Georgia. Under the program, workers were required to have their physicians submit a report directly to the medical department for all illnesses lasting over seven days. The medical department monitored the illness by keeping in contact with the employee, the supervisor, the attending physician, and the Personnel Department. The firm found that during the first year of the program there was a reduction of $237,000 in total sick leave expenditures.[18]

No-Fault Attendance Policies

A number of firms have attempted to reduce unscheduled absenteeism by using a "no-fault attendance policy." For example, the Kasei Memory Products Plant of Verbatim Corporation, a maker of computer disks, has a policy whereby employees are given points for missing work; these points result in prescribed penalties ranging from verbal warnings to termination. The more points an employee accumulates, the harsher the penalty.

Employees receive points for failure to work part or all of a scheduled workday, including scheduled and volunteered overtime. Tardiness, early departures, and leaving and returning to work during the same shift are also considered absences. Employees are not given any points for scheduled absences such as company holidays, jury duty, funeral leave, vacations, military leave, or injury absences.

Points are assigned in the following manner:

1. 1/2 point is given for any partial workday absence or late arrival of greater than 10 minutes or more but less than the half-day amount. Repeated tardiness of less than 10 minutes can also result in 1/2 point.

2. 1 point is assigned for one full day of absence with call-in before shift starts.

3. 1 1/2 points are given for one full day of absence with call-in after the shift begins.

4. 4 points are assigned for one full day of absence without call-in by the end of the shift.

The type of counseling given to offenders is directly related to the number of points earned. Employees who have received three points are given a verbal warning. Five points lead to a written warning. Eight points result in a suspension from work; and if an employee earns ten points within twelve months, the person is discharged.

However, prior to terminating any employee the immediate supervisor, the department manager, and the Manager of Human Resources make a review of possible extenuating circumstances. In addition, any employee who feels that an exception to the policy should be made has the right to file an appeal with a panel of at least four department managers.

Points earned by employees remain in their file for twelve months and are then removed. That is, on the twelfth-month anniversary of an absence, the points for that occurrence are deducted from the employee's cumulative attendance record and are not considered for corrective action purposes.

One other feature of Verbatim's policy involves an incentive for those having perfect attendance. Employees who experience no unscheduled absence for six consecutive months have their name and picture posted on the employee bulletin board. In addition, those who have no absences for one full calendar year receive a $25 mall gift certificate. Likewise, newly hired employees having perfect attendance for six months receive a $10 certificate, and those with nine months of perfect attendance receive $15.

Verbatim's policy is similar to that of most other firms in that it is designed to minimize unscheduled absences and tardiness. Its unique feature is that it combines rewards for perfect attendance with a no-fault disciplinary system. It has the benefit of eliminating the need to judge employee excuses for being absent or tardy. Regardless of the reason, employees earn points for an unscheduled absence. Furthermore, these points result in prescribed corrective actions, thereby insuring consistency across and within departments. Absenteeism records are maintained by the Human Resources Department, which informs the relevant department managers of the appropriate corrective action. Department managers are required to take action, thereby eliminating potential favoritism.

How successful has this approach been? According to the Manager of Human Resources at Verbatim,

This policy has reduced employee attendance problems. In prior years, there were employees who had high absenteeism. Their attendance has improved as the result of the new policy. We have found that on average employees miss approximately 40 hours per year. Coincidentally, that is what the company offers in annual sick/personal time. I believe that having a formal absenteeism policy makes employees accountable for their attendance. It keeps people honest, because they don't want to risk staying out when they are not really sick or have a legitimate reason.

Allen-Bradley Company in Fullerton, California, also has a no-fault policy. In this firm, all employees are counseled by the supervisor for any absenteeism. In addition, if an employee earns 6 points he/she receives a documented verbal warning. Nine points result in a formal written warning; 12, a three-day suspension; and 15, termination. Some absences do not lead to points (e.g., the first 40 hours of personal excused time, approved leaves of absence, military obligations, bereavement time, jury duty, workers' compensation leave, and vacations and holidays). Employees earn points in the following way:

Unreported absence	6 points
Absence reported before or within one hour after start of shift	3 points
Early leave or tardy	1 point

As was the case with Kasei Memory Products, points earned by employees are dropped off automatically after twelve months.

As a result of the no-fault policy, absenteeism has dropped by 83.5 percent over the first 25 months. This represents a total savings of $59,545, or $2,382 per month, exclusive of benefits and other hidden costs. Supervisors are pleased with the new policy, as are employees. Focus groups consisting of employees found that workers actually wanted the policy to be more strict, rather than more lenient.[19]

One apparent benefit is that no fault removes many of the angles abusers use to work the system. If, for example, a firm allows ten days of absence under its policy, the "sniper" will make sure that he/she has ten absences. This is especially true if the days are lost at the end of the year. Under no fault, the employee cannot do this because once someone accumulates a certain number of points, for whatever reason, he/she is disciplined.

Using Rewards

Many firms have relied on some form of rewards to improve employee attendance. Among these are praise, recognition awards, and prizes.

Recognition/Praise

Personal recognition for good attendance has been tried by numerous firms. This includes publicizing in the company newsletter/newspaper the names of employees who have perfect attendance, awarding an employee a perfect attendance certificate or plaque, sending a congratulatory letter, presenting rewards for attendance at a luncheon or dinner, and displaying a plaque showing the names of employees in the company lobby. Yet the Commerce Clearing House study[20] is not very supportive of this approach. Respondents viewed recognition programs as the least effective means of controlling absenteeism for hourly workers and ranked it fourth in effectiveness out of seven for salaried workers.

At least one study,[21] however, suggests that recognition programs can at times be effective. This study was conducted at the Maid Bess Corporation, a firm that operates "cut-and-sew" garment factories in southwestern Virginia and North Carolina. At the time of the study it employed 1,800 workers, 94 percent of whom were women.

The firm instituted a different absenteeism control program in each of its plants so that comparisons would be possible. In one plant, employees received a $50 cash bonus for perfect yearly attendance or a $25 bonus if only one or two days were missed. In another plant, a personal recognition program was instituted whereby employees with no more than one absence per quarter received a card signed by the manager notifying and congratulating them. Furthermore, employees who missed two or less days during the entire year received a custom-designed piece of engraved jewelry. In a third plant, a quarterly lottery program was instituted whereby a television or a mantle clock having a value of approximately $200 was awarded to the winner. If any employee had perfect attendance for the quarter, his/her name was entered twice. If the worker had one absence, his/her name was entered just once. Finally, a fourth plant instituted an information feedback program whereby employees received absenteeism feedback once a month with their paychecks. This indicated the employee's year-to-date attendance record, but no positive or negative connotation was attached to the information.

The results of the study showed that at the plant with the personal recognition program, absenteeism decreased by 36.9 percent, netting the firm $48,000 in direct labor costs after paying for the recognition awards. In addition, an employee survey showed that over 72 percent liked the program. It is interesting that absenteeism in the plant using financial incentives and in the one using information feedback dropped only slightly. The plant with the lottery actually experienced a slight increase in absenteeism. Thus, the study suggests that recognition programs may be more effective than many people think.

Rather than relying on recognition programs, some suggest that managers praise employees for attendance. For example, one air freight company suggests that employees who return from missing work the previous day be thanked, as outlined in the following conversation:

- *First Day*—"John, you came to work nineteen times out of twenty-two last month. When you're here we make more flights. Try to shoot for twenty-one or twenty-two days."
- *Second Day*—"Appreciate your coming to work today, John. Keep that up and you'll be here twenty-one or twenty-two days out of twenty-two."
- *Third Day*—"You've been here three days in a row now. Look at the percentage of flights we've made in the last three days. Keep shooting for twenty-one or twenty-two days."
- *Fifth Day*—"You've been here all week. Thank you, John. Only seventeen days to go for a perfect record this month."

In each case, the manager follows the procedure of rewarding the employee with praise and encouragement while reminding him of the company goals.

One of the greatest objections to the use of praise, recognition awards, and other incentives is that a manager is rewarding employees a second time for doing what they are supposed to do anyway. After all, people are paid for working; they have an obligation to be there. Why should there be additional incentives? Although this argument is very persuasive, one could argue that managers are paid to meet productivity goals and attendance is critical to this. If an additional reward to come to work regularly results in lower absenteeism, lower overall costs, and meeting production goals, then why not do it?

Poker/Lotteries

Games of chance have been used in an effort to improve attendance. These include lotteries, raffles, and poker games, among others. To illustrate, one unnamed manufacturing/distribution company devised a system whereby workers who arrived on time each day were allowed to draw a card from a deck. At the end of the week, those who were present all five days possessed a five-card stud poker hand. The company paid the high hand $20. There were eight winners, one for approximately each department. The game ran for around four months and then was discontinued. During that time absenteeism declined by 18 percent. Twenty-two weeks later the firm found that the absenteeism rate had returned to its original 3 percent.[22]

Leading Hardware used a lottery system to increase attendance among secretaries, sales and stock personnel, and porters. Each month, employees with perfect attendance and tardiness records were eligible to participate in a lottery drawing. A prize was awarded for every twenty-five employees. In addition, a second drawing for a major prize such as a color TV was held for employees who had perfect attendance records for six months. The results showed that sick leave payments were reduced by 62 percent and that absenteeism and tardiness decreased during the first year of the program by approximately 75 percent.[23]

A hospital tried two different lottery systems in an attempt to improve attendance among nurses, ward clerks, and nursing assistants. For one group of employees, workers who had no absences during a three-week period were eligible to participate in a cash prize drawing of $20. For a different group of employees, the hospital had a cash prize drawing for those who were present on eight dates randomly selected from the three-week period. The hospital found that absences declined in both groups, from 4.84 percent to 3.57 percent and from 4.19 percent to 2.65 percent, respectively.[24]

Although all three examples show that lotteries/games of chance can improve attendance, it is important to keep in mind that a study cited earlier found a slight increase in absences as a result of a lottery.[25] Thus, not all variable reward programs have proven to be effective. In any event, it appears that these programs are not too popular in industry. A survey of 987 personnel managers in 1982 found that only 1 percent used them.[26]

Bonuses for Attendance

Closely related to games of chance and recognition programs are bonuses for perfect attendance. The CCH study found that 21 percent of the 889 firms surveyed had bonus programs. Furthermore, bonuses were rated second for hourly workers and third for salaried workers in terms of effectively controlling absenteeism.[27]

Several firms have reported on their use of bonuses. In the Maid Bess Corporation study cited earlier in this chapter, a $50 bonus was paid to those who had perfect attendance for a year, whereas those with only one or two absences received $25. The company found that attendance improved only slightly (statistically nonsignificant) with this approach. On the other hand, some firms have found this approach to be effective. For example, at one firm having 142 production and office employees, $100 or forty hours of pay (whichever was greater) was given for perfect attendance over a six-month period. Less than perfect attendance was rewarded by $50 or twenty hours of pay. The firm found that absenteeism dropped from 2.47 percent to 1.53 percent for production workers and from 2.53 percent to 2.13 percent for office employees. Similarly, at a New York–based advertising agency where perfect attenders were given an extra week's pay at the end of the year, absenteeism decreased from 5.8 to 2.4 days per year.[28]

Paid Leave/Personal Time Banks

A paid leave bank combines various forms of paid leave into a set number of days and allows employees to control how those days are used. For example, one hospital allowed employees 12 sick leave days along with 10 vacation days and 6 holidays. It found that employee absences averaged less than the allocated sick leave days. Consequently, in establishing a personal time bank it allocated employees 24 days to be used in any way the employee chose, with the exception that five days had to be taken consecutively each year.[29]

Other firms have modified this approach. For example, some allot a specified number of days to a catastrophic illness account that would be used for prolonged illnesses of, say, five days or more. Others allow employees to periodically cash in unused leave time subject to a reasonable cap.

The paid leave bank is designed to reduce absenteeism in several ways. First, if employees miss work due to sickness, it may reduce the time they can spend on vacation. Thus, it may motivate those who have a minor illness or headache to come to work when they would otherwise stay home. At the same time, the paid leave bank financially rewards employees with good attendance records because they may be able to cash in some of their unused leave days. In essence, a paid leave bank may promote a "use it only when necessary" mindset for sick days rather than a "use it or lose it" attitude.[30]

Several studies have reported on the positive use of paid leave banks. In addition, the CCH study found that even though leave banks were the least used of the seven absence control programs surveyed, they were perceived by the almost 900 respondents to be the most effective tool to control sick leave abuse.

The results from the hospital's personal time bank program just described showed that after eighteen months the majority of employees (296, or 66%) felt that the program met or exceeded their needs, whereas 75 employees (34%) felt that it did not. The hospital also found that the time bank reduced unscheduled absences by 67 percent.[31]

A study conducted at a medical center found similarly favorable results.[32] Originally, the firm offered its employees ten to twenty days of vacation time depending on rank and length of service, seven holidays, and twelve days of sick leave per year. Under the leave bank system, vacation days, paid holidays, and five sick leave days were combined. The remaining seven sick leave days were assigned to a sick leave account. Employees could draw on their account at will and could cash out part of it periodically. The sick leave account was intended for long-term illness and could be used only after the paid leave account was exhausted. The new plan rewarded employees with longer vacations or cash payments for reducing casual absences. On the other hand, absences of more than five days reduced what was formerly holidays and vacation days. The medical center found that paid sick hours ranged between 12 and 22 percent of sick hours earned for a period of two and a half years after introducing the leave program; this was down significantly from 65 percent previously.

Finally, Hewlett-Packard found that within one year of introducing a paid leave bank policy, average annual sick time decreased from 34 to 22 hours per employee. The firm stresses that employees should set aside several days for unexpected illnesses, because they are not paid for the first five days taken once their leave bank is depleted. (After that, short-term disability coverage begins.)[33]

Well-Pay Programs

An additional option would be to use a well-pay program designed to offer employees a monetary incentive for perfect or near-perfect attendance. For example, one nonprofit organization with 120 employees implemented a plan whereby employees with perfect attendance (no sickness) for four consecutive weeks would receive a bonus of four hours' pay. They also discontinued the current accrual of sick leave and discontinued paying for the first eight hours of absence due to illness. One year after the plan was introduced the firm surveyed its employees and found that even though many did not like it, the program was still preferable to the previous sick leave plan. On the other hand, supervisors were quite satisfied with the well-pay plan: 85 percent indicated they were moderately or very satisfied. They believed it was somewhat more effective in increasing productivity and reducing absenteeism than the sick leave system. Indeed, a review of absenteeism statistics revealed that unscheduled absences actually decreased 45.5 percent. Moreover, the well-pay program was found to be slightly less expensive than the sick leave plan even though the firm paid $38,000 in bonuses.[34]

COUNSELING EMPLOYEES FOR ABSENTEEISM

Whichever approach for controlling absenteeism is used, most managers are still faced with the problem of counseling employees for absenteeism. This is particularly true when a worker's attendance is currently unsatisfactory or is satisfactory now but definitely heading in the wrong direction. How should the issue be approached? One method is to counsel the employee and use a three-phase strategy.

Diagnosing the Problem

There are a multitude of reasons why workers are absent, so the manager's initial goal is to determine in a nonthreatening way the major reason or reasons. This can be accomplished by getting the employee to talk freely about the problem, thereby discovering if there is an underlying problem that should be addressed.

Developing an Action Plan

Once the reason for the absenteeism becomes clear, an action plan to solve the problem can be developed. It is important to let the employee take an active role in the plan's development because a sense of ownership will improve commitment and acceptance. If an employee is given a plan that does not reflect his/her own ideas, the worker will be more inclined to question its validity and be less committed to making it work.[35]

Some employees are absent because they don't clearly understand the firm's attendance policy, whereas others don't view attendance as very important. In these situations, the manager must explain the policy and/or stress the importance of good attendance, being sure to spell out the negative outcomes that result from chronic absenteeism. The supervisor may even want to show the employee how important his/her job is to others in an effort to increase the person's self-esteem and motivation.

Other employees are sporadically absent for medical or psychological reasons. These problems may require that the employee be referred to a professional for treatment, and a leave of absence from work may be needed if the employee's problem cannot be resolved quickly. On the other hand, employees who are absent because of job dissatisfaction or because of conflicts with coworkers may need to be dismissed or transferred to a new position.

As the Family and Medical Leave Act comes more into play, employees who are absent due to childbirth, family difficulties involving illness, or personal serious illness will need to be accommodated. At this point, it is not clear what options an employer may have other than generally allowing the unpaid leave and covering the employees' positions until they can return.

Evaluating Results/Reinforcing Improvement

Once a manager and employee have reached an agreement regarding steps that will be taken to improve attendance, the third phase involves monitoring the situation to see how well the plan is working. Keeping careful attendance records and talking frequently with the employee is a good first step. In addition, giving systematic praise for improved attendance may help to further improve the person's behavior.

CONCLUSION

Although employee absenteeism is a major problem in many firms, managers have the ability to control it if they are willing to give it priority. That is, instead of simply complaining about the problem, managers must approach the problem systematically and find long-term solutions that fit the particular culture and needs of the organization.[36]

In this chapter we have presented numerous strategies that managers can use to control absenteeism and have described specific examples of how firms have implemented them. These include taking disciplinary action, developing a no-fault attendance policy, using rewards, instituting paid leave banks, and implementing a well-pay program. These policies all focus on trying to change the employee's motivation to attend. However, absenteeism may result from an employee's inability to come to work. Different approaches are needed to solve this problem, such as establishing day care centers, offering stress management or wellness programs, giving employees the opportunity to work flexible schedules, creating carpools, and designing interesting and enriching jobs. These approaches are beyond the scope of this book.

In dealing with absenteeism problems, all managers are constrained to some extent by their own firm's policies and by the new federal law. Nonetheless, there are some things that managers can do on their own, regardless of the firm's policy. For example:

- When interviewing job applicants, evaluate each in terms of probable attendance and punctuality. What has their attendance record been in the past?
- During new employee orientation, stress the importance of attendance. Explain the attendance policy thoroughly and emphasize the importance of coming to work. Make sure the employees understand that they are an integral part of the firm, regardless of size.
- Remind employees periodically that attendance is important. Indicate that it is considered when making pay and promotion decisions.
- Document absences as soon as they occur. Periodically analyze attendance patterns. Are employees missing Fridays, Mondays, days after payday, or days near paid holidays? Are employees on certain jobs or working for particular supervisors more frequently absent?
- When an absent employee returns to work, follow the counseling approach mentioned in this chapter. That is, determine the reason for the absence, develop a solution, and monitor future attendance.
- Plan ahead so that if an employee is absent, a replacement is available. This may entail the use of cross-training and preparing a list of substitutes who can fill in.
- Consistently follow the firm's attendance policy. Don't ignore it or look the other way when some are absent but follow it with others.

NOTES

1. "Quarterly Report on Job Absence and Turnover," *Bureau of National Affairs*, March 11, 1993.

2. P. Goodman and R. Atkin, *Absenteeism: New Approaches to Understanding, Measuring, and Managing Employee Absence* (San Francisco: Jossey-Bass, 1984).

3. "CCH Absence Survey," *Commerce Clearing House*, February 20, 1991, pp. 1–4.

4. R. A. Bula, "Absenteeism Control," *Personnel Journal*, June 1984, pp. 56–60.

5. "CCH Absence Survey."

6. Ibid.

7. Ibid.

8. J. R. Redeker, *Employee Discipline: Policies and Practices* (Washington, DC: Bureau of National Affairs, 1989).

9. Automotive Distributors, 76 LA 552.

10. Champion International, 74 LA 623.

11. Menasha Corp., 71 LA 653.

12. 77 LA 1049, 1052.

13. 91-1 ARB 8150.

14. Redeker, *Employee Discipline: Policies and Practices.*

15. S. R. Rhodes and R. M. Steers, *Managing Employee Absenteeism* (Reading, MA: Addison-Wesley Publishing, 1990).

16. "CCH Absence Survey."

17. J. E. Ford, "A Simple Punishment Procedure for Controlling Employee Absenteeism," *Journal of Organizational Behavior Management* 3, no. 2 (1981), pp. 71–79.

18. K. T. Woodsides, "Yes, Management, Your Medical Department Can Affect the Bottom Line," *Journal of Occupational Medicine* 22, no. 4 (1980), pp. 232–234.

19. J. Stinson, "Company Policy Attends to Chronic Absentees," *Personnel Journal*, August 1991, pp. 12–14.

20. "CCH Absence Survey."

21. K. D. Scott, S. E. Markham, and R. W. Robers, "Rewarding Good Attendance: A Comparative Study of Positive Ways to Reduce Absenteeism," *Personnel Administrator*, August 1985, pp. 72–83.

22. E. Pedalino and V. U. Gamboa, "Behavior Modification and Absenteeism: Intervention in One Industrial Setting," *Journal of Applied Psychology* 59 (1974), pp. 694–698.

23. W. R. Nord, "Improving Attendance through Rewards," *Personnel Administration* 33, no. 6 (1970), pp. 37–41.

24. T. A. Stephens and W. A. Burroughs, "An Application of Operant Conditioning to Absenteeism in a Hospital Setting," *Journal of Applied Psychology* 63 (1978), pp. 518–521.

25. Scott et al., "Rewarding Good Attendance."

26. D. Scott and S. Markham, "Absenteeism Control Methods: A Survey of Practices and Results," *Personnel Administrator* 27, no. 6 (1982), pp. 73–84.

27. "CCH Absence Survey."

28. Rhodes and Steers, *Managing Employee Absenteeism.*

29. B. H. Harvey, "Two Alternatives to Traditional Sick Leave Programs," *Personnel Journal*, May 1983, pp. 374–378.

30. "CCH Absence Survey."

31. Harvey, "Two Alternatives to Traditional Sick Leave Programs."

32. R. E. Kopelman, G. O. Schneller, and J. J. Silver, "Parkinson's Law and Absenteeism: A Program to Rein in Sick Leave Costs," *Personnel Administrator* 26, no. 5 (1981), pp. 57–64.

33. D. Michals, "Solution for Employee Absenteeism," *Working Woman*, June 1991, p. 24.

34. Harvey, "Two Alternatives to Traditional Sick Leave Programs."

35. D. L. Kennedy, "A Counseling Approach to Chronic Tardiness," *Supervisory Management*, November 1984, pp. 25–29.

36. Rhodes and Steers, *Managing Employee Absenteeism.*

Chapter 8

Dealing with Improper Interpersonal Conduct

John Moore is one of the best and most productive members in the industrial sales department of a firm supplying products to automobile assembly plants. Having been with the company for over twenty years, he has several large and important accounts that he handles personally.

In the field of industrial sales, close relations between the customer and sales representative are fairly common. Because there is not a huge difference in the quality among most industrial products, the company that prevails has to rely on the ability of its sales representatives to establish good rapport with the customers. Sales are often based on respect and friendship, so representatives are frequently able to take accounts with them if they move to another firm. As a result, the sales manager has given the representatives considerable autonomy and seems willing to tolerate some fairly raucous behaviors within the office itself.

On one recent occasion, a young female secretary made a mistake in a proposal that Moore sent to a potential new customer. Upon discovering the error, Moore, who is normally friendly and outgoing with the office staff, stormed into the work area where the secretary was located and, in front of others, delivered an explosion of expletives. She ran out of the area on the verge of tears and later, in conference with the supervisor of clerical staff, threatened to leave the company, saying that she would not tolerate such outbursts by Moore or any other sales representative. No job could be worth that kind of personal abuse. She demanded that Moore be issued an official reprimand, and if no such action was taken, she would file a grievance.

When he was presented with this ultimatum, the sales manager was upset. How could he reprimand a top sales representative over this incident without risking the loss of this person to another company? On the other hand, the grievance would not look good to top management, who might force him to take action anyway. What should he do?

In this incident we see how inappropriate and offensive interaction between employees has the potential to damage the morale and effectiveness of an organization. In some situations the problem may be that employees are exercising very poor taste and judgment in dealing with others. The conduct is not likely to lead to grievances or litigation, but it is clearly not professional. At times, however, the conduct can become so offensive that the workplace environment becomes hostile and intimidating. In that case the firm may find itself answering allegations of unlawful harassment.

In this chapter we focus on three examples of improper interpersonal conduct: sexual or other forms of unlawful harassment, affairs and other romantic escapades at work, and the unrestrained use of vulgar language on the job. In each area we discuss why the behavior is a problem, policies that may help the organization to preempt the offense, and actions a firm might take in addressing the behavior.

UNLAWFUL HARASSMENT

Suppose that an employee who is a supervisor or manager goes out of his way to stare at a female subordinate every time she walks by his desk. What if he makes remarks about her body or clothing? Let's say that the supervisor constantly tells sexually suggestive jokes in the presence of women or uses racial or ethnic slurs when talking to or referring to an employee. Let's say that he doesn't do anything directly but allows other employees to post sexually graphic cartoons or pictures and then refuses to take action when someone complains about them. In all these situations the organization could be risking a charge of sexual or some other form of illegal harassment, which is a violation of section 703 of Title VII (Civil Rights Act of 1964). In addition, it would be facing legal action under the widely recognized tort, intentional infliction of emotional distress.

Prevalence of Harassment

In recent years, significant attention has been directed toward understanding and eliminating unlawful sexual harassment in the workplace. Even though this is not a new problem, it was the October 1991 hearings involving Anita Hill and Clarence Thomas, before the U.S. Senate Judiciary Committee, that brought the issues into full focus. In the wake of these proceedings, virtually every newspaper and magazine across the country published extensive articles on sexual harassment. They raised questions regarding how to define harassment, how to determine when it has occurred, and what actions should be taken to prevent it. But long before this happened, various studies had documented the serious nature of the problem. For example, the U.S. Merit Systems Protection Board (MSPB) studied 23,000 employees in 1981 and found that 42 percent of the females reported experiencing some form of sexual harassment. Most of the females reporting harassment were young and the alleged harassers were older, married males. Even though harassers were more likely to be coworkers than supervisors, serious forms of harassment were more likely to be attributed to supervisors.[1]

Results of the MSPB survey supported earlier reports that attempted to quantify the effects of sexual harassment on employee productivity. According to the findings, harassment of employees cost the taxpayers approximately $267 million over a two-year period. Included in these figures were costs of training new employees, costs of treating the health problems of the harassed employees, and costs of absenteeism and lost productivity.

A more recent government survey reinforces these findings. In a major study of sexual harassment in the military, the Pentagon found that more than one-third of the women surveyed experienced some form of direct harassment including touching, pressure for sex, and rape. In all, 64 percent of the women surveyed said they had been harassed, either directly or in more subtle ways (e.g., by catcalls, dirty looks, and teasing). In addition, 17 percent of the men surveyed said that they had been sexually harassed by male or female colleagues.[2] Clearly, the problem is real.

Sexual Harassment Defined

What constitutes sexual harassment? One author defines it as "unsolicited non-reciprocal male behavior that asserts a woman's sex role over her function as worker."[3] Another writer says it is sexual activity that is "one-sided, unwelcomed, or comes with strings attached."[4] In guidelines issued by the Equal Employment Opportunity Commission (see Exhibit 8.1), three criteria are cited that constitute unlawful behavior. According to the EEOC, harassment involves the following:

Unwelcome sexual advances, requests for sexual favors, and other verbal or physical conduct of a sexual nature when (1) submission to such conduct is made either explicitly or implicitly a term or condition of an individual's employment; (2) submission to or rejection of such conduct by an individual is used as a basis for employment decisions affecting the individual; or (3) such conduct has the purpose or effect of unreasonably interfering with an individual's work performance or creating an intimidating, hostile, or offensive work environment.

The problem for management is that although the EEOC guidelines are clear in terms of intent, they fall short when it comes to the detail. They place an employer on notice that sexual harassment cannot be tolerated and if such behavior exists and management does not make every effort

Exhibit 8.1
The EEOC's Interim Guidelines on Sexual Harassment

PART 1604—GUIDELINES ON DISCRIMINATION
BECAUSE OF SEX
Section 1604.11 Sexual harassment.

a) Harassment on the basis of sex is a violation of Sec. 703 of Title VII. Unwelcome sexual advances, requests for sexual favors, and other verbal or physical conduct of a sexual nature constitute sexual harassment when—

(1) submission to such conduct is made either explicitly or implicitly a term or condition of an individual's employment,

(2) submission to or rejection of such conduct by an individual is used as the basis for employment decisions affecting such individuals, or

(3) such conduct has the purpose or effect of substantially interfering with an individual's work performance or creating an intimidating, hostile, or offensive working environment.

b) In determining whether alleged conduct constitutes sexual harassment, the commission will look at the record as a whole and the totality of the circumstances such as the nature of the sexual advances and the context in which the alleged incidents occurred. The determination of the legality of the particular action will be made from the facts on a case-by-case basis.

c) Applying general Title VII principles, an employer, employment agency, joint apprenticeship committee, or labor organization (hereinafter collectively referred to as "employer") is responsible for its acts and those of its agents and supervisory employees with respect to sexual harassment regardless of whether the specific acts complained of were authorized or even forbidden by the employer and regardless of whether the employer knew or should have known of their occurrence. The Commission will examine the circumstances of the particular employment relationship and the job functions performed by the individual in determining whether an individual acts in either a supervisory or agency capacity.

d) With respect to persons other than those mentioned in subsection (c) above, an employer is responsible for acts of sexual harassment in the workplace where the employer, or its agents or supervisory employees, knows or should have known of the conduct. An employer may rebut apparent liability for such acts by showing that it took immediate and appropriate corrective action.

e) Prevention is the best tool for the elimination of sexual harassment. An employer should take all steps necessary to prevent sexual harassment from occurring such as affirmatively raising the subject, expressing strong disapproval, developing appropriate sanctions, informing employees of their right to raise and how to raise the issue of harassment under Title VII, and developing methods to sensitize all concerned.

---

to eliminate it, then the organization faces serious legal liabilities. How should this be accomplished?

Court Rulings

By far the most important court ruling is the June 1986 U.S. Supreme Court decision in *Meritor Savings Bank v. Vinson.*[5] The plaintiff in this case, Mechelle Vinson, had worked for branch manager Sidney Taylor since 1974, first as a trainee, then as head teller, and eventually as assistant branch manager. It was undisputed that her promotions were based on merit, and along the way she received good pay raises. Yet in 1978, approximately two months after she notified Taylor that she would be taking an indefinite period of sick leave, she was fired for excessive use of sick leave.

After her dismissal Vinson brought suit under Title VII, charging that during three of her four years at the bank she was constantly subjected to unwanted sexual advances from Taylor, including forty or fifty acts of sexual intercourse, being fondled in front of other employees, and frequently being followed into the restroom. Vinson had never reported Taylor's conduct to any senior manager, nor had she attempted to use the bank's complaint procedure. Therefore, senior management knew nothing of the alleged behavior and, of course, no attempt was made to discipline Taylor.

When the case went to court, the attorneys for Meritor argued that the firm could not be held liable because Vinson had never informed anyone in authority. The U.S. Court of Appeals for the D.C. Circuit disagreed, however, and ruled that the bank was indeed liable even though none of the top executives had any direct or indirect knowledge of the branch manager's behavior. The court held that because Taylor was an agent for the bank, he bound the firm in his lawful dealings with employees and also in any unlawful act of harassment. Therefore, whether or not Vinson filed a formal complaint was not relevant. Clearly, this put Meritor Savings in a very difficult position.

When the case was brought before the U.S. Supreme Court, the Justices were asked to rule on three issues:[6]

1. Whether a hostile work environment (where the hostility is because of the victim's gender) in which the victim does not suffer any economic loss violates Title VII;

2. Whether an employee's voluntary participation in sexual acts with a manager constitutes a valid defense for an employer; and

3. Whether an employer is liable for the conduct of supervisors and coworkers when the harassment has never been reported to senior management and the employer is unaware of the conduct.

The majority decision clearly addressed the first two issues. The Court ruled that Title VII is not limited to discrimination resulting in tangible economic loss. An employee can be given raises and promotions and yet feel that the work environment is hostile, intimidating, and offensive. In terms of the second issue, the Court ruled that the appropriate test is not whether the employee voluntarily engaged in sexual intercourse and activity with her manager, but whether the sexual activity was unwelcomed and uninvited.

When it came to the third issue involving employer liability for actions of which it was unaware, the Court was split; the majority declined to issue a definitive ruling. They said that agency principles should be used on a case-by-case basis when determining liability. At the same time, however, the majority rejected the bank's argument that the existence of a grievance procedure and a specific policy against discrimination, coupled with the employee's failure to use the procedure, insulates the employer from legal action.

The Court pointed out that in this case the bank's policy against harassment did not mention sexual harassment, and its grievance procedure required the employee to go first to the immediate supervisor, who happened to be doing the harassing. The majority said that management's arguments would have been much stronger if its published policy against harassment and its grievance system encouraged victims to come forward by allowing employees to bypass their supervisor.

For a variety of reasons, this is an extremely important ruling. It holds that an employer has a responsibility to know what is going on and to provide employees with a complaint procedure that allows them to come forward without fear of recrimination.

In the wake of the *Vinson* decision, other federal court rulings have attempted to further define the legal principles associated with sexual harassment. If the harassment is quid pro quo (i.e., the employee suffers economic loss because of resistance to a supervisor's sexual advances or other misconduct), the firm will always be liable. However, when the complaint involves a charge of hostile working environment, there is room for interpretation and discussion.

As a general rule, a hostile environment exists whenever the harassment is so severe or pervasive that it alters the conditions of employment and creates a hostile work situation. If remarks or behavior are, in the Court's view, occasional, isolated, or trivial, it is not likely that the requirement of pervasiveness will be satisfied. For example, in *Jones v. Flagship International*[7] the sexual advances by one of the employer's vice presidents, and the sculpting of bare-breasted mermaids by the employers' executive chef as table decorations for an office Christmas party, were held by the Fifth Circuit Court to be insufficiently pervasive to constitute a hostile work environment. Similarly, in *Vermouth v. Hugh*[8] the District Court for the Western District of Michigan rejected a claim of hostile work environment brought by a female state trooper. Rather, said the court, the complained-of conduct was the sort of routine teasing that any new recruit (male or female) would have encountered. In addition, factors that need to be considered in order to determine whether an abusive work environment exists are as follows: the nature of the unwelcome sexual acts or words, the frequency of offensive encounters, the total number of days over which all the offensive meetings occur, and the context in which the sexually harassing conduct occurred. Nevertheless, acts or words that occur over a short time period can lead to legal action if there is a consistent pattern and the harassment is sufficiently intense. Finally, following the ruling in *Ellison v. Brady*, most courts now measure offensiveness on the basis of an objective standard keyed to a "reasonable woman" in determining whether a female plaintiff has presented a prima facie case of hostile work environment. Although sexual harassment need not be psychologically disabling, it must, under the objective standard, be significant enough that an average female employee would find her overall work performance substantially and adversely affected by the conduct.[9]

To make matters even more complex, a recent decision by the U.S. District Court for Rhode Island (in *Showalter v. Allison Reed Group*) permitted recovery under both quid pro quo and hostile working environment for two male employees.[10] The plaintiffs in this unusual case charged that they were forced to observe their boss having sex with his secretary. This involved sexual intercourse as well as other acts such as watching an after-hours strip tease orchestrated by the supervisor and performed by the secretary. Furthermore, the plaintiffs themselves were allegedly ordered to engage in sexual activities in the office of the secretary while the boss watched them from an adjoining room. In all instances, plaintiffs contended that they participated because they feared they would lose their jobs if they did not comply with the sexual demands and orders of the supervisor. In fact, following their separation from the company, the plaintiffs did claim that the supervisor had threatened to fire them.

Finally, as we saw in Chapter 2 in *Holland v. First Virginia Banks*, harassment is not limited to that based on gender. In the near future, firms will almost surely be faced with lawsuits in which employees charge they have been harassed as a result of race, handicapped status, age, religion, or ethnic background. Certainly, nothing in the language of any federal civil rights statute would lead one to conclude that these other forms of harassment could not become a viable cause for action. We therefore argue that organizations must become more aware of the issues and begin to implement policies and practices that will prevent serious problems from developing.

Dealing with Unlawful Harassment

What can a firm do to effectively deal with harassment? The Equal Employment Opportunity Commission (EEOC) guidelines, as shown in

Exhibit 8.1, state that prevention is the best tool. An employer should take all necessary steps to see that harassment does not occur, including the following:

- Affirmatively raising the subject;
- Expressing strong disapproval of sexual harassment;
- Developing appropriate sanctions for offenders;
- Informing employees of their rights under Title VII; and
- Developing methods to sensitize employees about sexual harassment in the organization.

All these steps are important, but they do not offer specific advice. As a result, firms have generally been left to their own devices and have responded to the guidelines in a variety of ways. A few have actually tried to ignore them. Others have merely given them lip service. However, most medium- and large-sized firms appear to have taken the guidelines seriously and have developed specific policies and programs to enlighten employees and to sanction offenders. They have provided training and have used other informational devices to sensitize all employees to sexual harassment and to inform them of their rights and responsibilities. In addition, grievance procedures have been changed so that victims can report complaints to someone other than their immediate supervisor; and when the evidence of misconduct is strong, offenders are generally subject to immediate discharge.

However, these steps, although necessary, may not be sufficient. In fact, we argue that these programs and policies are rarely evaluated in a systematic way. Most firms do not know whether supervisors and managers clearly understand sexual harassment in terms of specific behaviors and whether their behavior reflects this understanding.

Conducting a Harassment Audit

One approach to addressing the problem is to conduct a sexual harassment audit. This proactive approach involves a straightforward, three-step procedure.[11] The *first step* is for the firm to develop a questionnaire such as the one shown in Exhibit 8.2 which attempts to determine whether managers understand what behaviors could be sexual harassment. Similar questionnaires may be developed for other types of harassment (e.g., racial, ethic, religious).

Once the questionnaire has been developed, the *second step* is to pretest it. The purpose is to identify ambiguous questions and develop a more reliable, accurate, and comprehensive evaluation instrument. As a *third step*, the final questionnaire is administered to either a random sample or

Exhibit 8.2
Sample Questionnaire

Situation (Part A)	Would it be Sexual Harassment?			Are you currently aware of or have you recently observed this behavior within the organization?	
	Yes	No	Uncertain	Yes	No
1. Mr. (Ms.) X (Supervisor) habitually posts cartoons on a certain bulletin board containing sexual related materials.	Yes	No	Uncertain	Yes	No
2. Mr. (Ms.) X (Supervisor) constantly tells sexually related jokes to female (male) subordinates. They seem to share his (her) sense of humor.	Yes	No	Uncertain	Yes	No
3. Mr. (Ms.) X (Supervisor) asks a female (male) subordinate for a date which she (he) willingly accepts.	Yes	No	Uncertain	Yes	No
4. Mr. (Ms.) X (Supervisor) enjoys patting or pinching female (male) subordinates as a way of providing encouragement.	Yes	No	Uncertain	Yes	No
5. Mr. (Ms.) X (Supervisor) kisses a female (male) subordinate on the cheek when wishing her (him) a happy birthday.	Yes	No	Uncertain	Yes	No
6. Mr. (Ms.) X (Supervisor) often touches subordinates on the shoulder when talking to them.	Yes	No	Uncertain	Yes	No

Exhibit 8.2 (continued)

Situation (Part A)	Would it be Sexual Harassment?			Are you currently aware of or have you recently observed this behavior within the organization?	
	Yes	No	Uncertain	Yes	No
7. Mr. (Ms.) X (Supervisor) brushes up against a female (male) subordinate whenever he (she) passes by her (him) in the hallway.	Yes	No	Uncertain	Yes	No
8. Mr. (Ms.) X (Supervisor) terminates a female (male) subordinate for not complying with his (her) requests for sexual favors. He (she) has recently given the subordinate a positive performance appraisal.	Yes	No	Uncertain	Yes	No
9. Mr. (Ms.) X (Supervisor) has on several occasions, had sexual intercourse with a female (male) on and off company premises.	Yes	No	Uncertain	Yes	No
10. Mr. (Ms.) X (Supervisor) posts a wall calendar in his (her) office that shows female (male) models clad in skimpy swim suits.	Yes	No	Uncertain	Yes	No
11. Mr. (Ms.) X (Supervisor) denies a raise to a female (male) subordinate soon after he (she) is turned down on a request to meet for dinner.	Yes	No	Uncertain	Yes	No
12. Mr. (Ms.) X (Supervisor) has a habit of staring at a female (male) subordinate whenever she (he) walks past his (her) desk.	Yes	No	Uncertain	Yes	No

136

#	Item	Yes	No	Uncertain	Yes	No	Uncertain
13.	Mr. (Ms.) X (Supervisor) in the presence of others often asks a female (male) secretary to "Be a good girl (boy) and get coffee".	Yes	No	Uncertain	Yes	No	Uncertain
14.	Mr. X (Supervisor) habitually calls all female employees "sweetie" or "honey."	Yes	No	Uncertain	Yes	No	Uncertain
15.	Mr. (Ms.) X (Supervisor) takes the female (male) secretary to lunch on "Secretaries' Day".	Yes	No	Uncertain	Yes	No	Uncertain
16.	Mr. (Ms.) X (Supervisor) often asks a female (male) employee for her (his) opinion regarding issues such as sex education courses taught in public schools in their town.	Yes	No	Uncertain	Yes	No	Uncertain
17.	Mr. X (Supervisor) recommends that a female subordinate wear revealing attire at work because a particular client likes people to be dressed that way.	Yes	No	Uncertain	Yes	No	Uncertain
18.	Mr. (Ms.) X (Supervisor) fails to promote a female (male) subordinate for not granting sexual favors.	Yes	No	Uncertain	Yes	No	Uncertain
19.	Mr. (Ms.) X (Supervisor) sends the book, "Joys of Sex" to a female (male) subordinate as a gag gift.	Yes	No	Uncertain	Yes	No	Uncertain

Exhibit 8.2 (continued)

Situation (Part A)	Would it be Sexual Harassment?			Are you currently aware of or have you recently observed this behavior within the organization?	
	Yes	No	Uncertain	Yes	No
20. Mr. (Ms.) X (Supervisor) invites a female (male) subordinate to accompany him (her) on a two-day business meeting in another city.	Yes	No	Uncertain	Yes	No
21. Mr. X (Supervisor) seems to lean and peer over the back of a female employee whenever she wears a low cut dress.	Yes	No	Uncertain	Yes	No
22. Mr. (Ms.) X (Supervisor) tells a female (male) job applicant that she (he) won't be hired unless she (he) agrees to have sexual intercourse.	Yes	No	Uncertain	Yes	No
23. Mr. X (Supervisor) frequently rolls up the sleeves on his long sleeve shirt at meetings attended by female subordinates.	Yes	No	Uncertain	Yes	No
24. Mr. (Ms.) X (Supervisor) gives a subordinate a substantial raise even though she (he) has repeatedly rejected the bosses' sexual overtures. The subordinate files a grievance charging sexual harassment.	Yes	No	Uncertain	Yes	No
25. Mr. (Ms.) X (Supervisor) gives a female (male) subordinate a nice present on her (his) birthday.	Yes	No	Uncertain	Yes	No

138

26.	Mr. (Ms.) X (Supervisor) asks a female employee to massage his (her) shoulders.	Yes No	Uncertain	Yes	No
27.	Mr. X (Supervisor) looks up the skirt of a female subordinate who often wears her skirt short. He has not made remarks or improper advances toward her.	Yes No	Uncertain	Yes	No
28.	Mr. (Ms.) X (supervisor) follows a female (male) subordinate into the women's (men's) bathroom.	Yes No	Uncertain	Yes	No
29.	Mr. X (Supervisor) frequently walks around the work area where women are present with his fly unzipped.	Yes No	Uncertain	Yes	No
30.	Mr. (Ms.) X (Supervisor) invites a female (male) to meet him (her) at a bar which features female (male) exotic dancers.	Yes No	Uncertain	Yes	No
31.	Mr. X (Supervisor) takes his shirt off while playing volleyball at a company party. Female employees are playing volleyball too.	Yes No	Uncertain	Yes	No

139

Exhibit 8.2 (continued)

Situation (Part A)	Would it be Sexual Harassment?			Are you currently aware of or have you recently observed this behavior within the organization?	
	Yes	No	Uncertain	Yes	No
32. Mr. (Ms.) X (Supervisor) likes to play comedy tapes that feature obscene language and jokes that are clearly derogatory toward the opposite sex. Female (male) subordinates can hear the radio through the twin wall but, to date, nobody has complained.	Yes	No	Uncertain	Yes	No
33. Mr. X (Supervisor) is writing a memo and asks a female secretary how to spell the word, "brassiere".	Yes	No	Uncertain	Yes	No
34. Mr. (Ms.) X (Supervisor) stands very close to a female (male) subordinate whenever talking to her (him).	Yes	No	Uncertain	Yes	No
35. Mr. X (Supervisor) hires an authentic belly dancer to perform at the firm's Christmas party attended by all employees.	Yes	No	Uncertain	Yes	No
36. Mr. (Ms.) X (Supervisor) invites a female (male) subordinate and a few of her (his) friends to come over to his (her) apartment for a hot tub party.	Yes	No	Uncertain	Yes	No
37. Mr. (Ms.) X (Supervisor) repeatedly asks a female (male) employee about her (his) love life.	Yes	No	Uncertain	Yes	No

		Yes	No	Uncertain		Yes	No
38.	Mr. (Ms.) X (Supervisor) sends his (her) secretary a birthday card that features a backside view of a naked person.	Yes	No	Uncertain		Yes	No
39.	Mr. X (Supervisor) tells a female employee that she must wear tight clothing for safety reasons.	Yes	No	Uncertain		Yes	No
40.	Mr. X (Supervisor) walks up to a group of subordinates who are talking about sexual harassment and jokingly says, "I wish someone would harass me".	Yes	No	Uncertain		Yes	No

Exhibit 8.2 (continued)

Situation (Part B)	Would it be Sexual Harassment?			Are you currently aware of or have you recently observed this behavior within the Organization?	
	Yes	No	Uncertain	Yes	No
1. A male clerk asks a female clerk for a date which she refuses. He decides to keep asking until she says yes.	Yes	No	Uncertain	Yes	No
2. Male (female) workers whistle everytime female (male) employees walk by their work area.	Yes	No	Uncertain	Yes	No
3. A married female employee and a married male employer are having an affair.	Yes	No	Uncertain	Yes	No
4. Male employees repeatedly use vulgar language when talking to each other. Two female employees often overhear what is said and find it offensive.	Yes	No	Uncertain	Yes	No
5. A male repair technician who works for another firm asks female employees for dates every time he comes to repair equipment. They always say no but he persists anyway.	Yes	No	Uncertain	Yes	No

all managers. The data can easily be analyzed using descriptive statistics, such as frequency distributions and correlations.

Taking Corrective Action

Depending on the survey results, various corrective actions may be warranted. If many managers say they do not understand the policy or cannot identify behaviors that are clearly or very likely to be harassment, then instituting new training programs or modifying current training efforts may be necessary. Alternatively, a firm could send out a special newsletter, brochures, or memos that clarify misunderstandings and make this information part of its new employee orientation. Meetings between the firm's Equal Employment Opportunity (EEO) compliance officers and selected departments or supervisors may also be appropriate or required.

In the event the questionnaire reveals that employees are currently aware of sexual harassment within the firm, top management and/or human resource specialists must take immediate action to stop the illegal behavior and correct the situations that precipitated it. In most cases, anyone who is engaging in any form of harassment, including seemingly minor incidents, should receive a strong warning. When the behavior is blatant, immediate dismissal may be appropriate.

According to the government surveys cited earlier, most cases of sexual harassment are subtle and involve sexual teasing, jokes, remarks, suggestive looks or gestures, touching, and leaning over a person. Outright assault or demands for sexual favors in return for hiring, promotions, and raises are less prevalent. According to James Lafferty, spokesperson for the Office of Personnel Management, most people do not take these lesser infractions seriously enough to report them. For example, only approximately 5 percent of those who said they had been harassed had actually filed an official complaint.[12] The rest apparently took matters into their own hands or said nothing in the hope that the problem would resolve itself. Nevertheless, if employees are unwilling to come forward voluntarily, the *Vinson* decision essentially places the burden on the company to seek out information and take corrective action. Opting for a "see no evil" approach probably will not work in court.

A human resources audit instrument can be effective in eliciting the necessary information from employees. The questionnaire gives the firm the early warning it needs and, in the event that a harassment complaint is made, provides evidence of a good-faith effort to eradicate the offensive behavior. Employers who use human resources auditing stand a greater chance of avoiding harassment suits and, should they arise, are better positioned to defend against them.

Developing a Policy of Mutual Respect

Another way for a firm to address harassment involves the development of a Policy of Mutual Respect, as shown in Exhibit 8.3. Essentially this

Exhibit 8.3
Policy of Mutual Respect

A primary mission of XYZ Chemical Co. is to promote a spirit of teamwork and cooperation among all of its employees. Furthermore, we wish to achieve a psychologically healthy work environment, one in which people feel mutually respected. To achieve these goals, we ask that all employees treat their coworkers, supervisors, and subordinates with the respect, honesty, consideration, and cooperation they seek from them. More specifically, we ask that each employee refrain from making statements that others will potentially find upsetting and create a hostile working environment. These particularly include kidding remarks, jokes, and hazing statements directed at another's age, sex, race, religion, national origin, or physical appearance. Although these statements are often not intended to be harmful, the effects can be detrimental. This policy is intended as a guide for maintaining effective interpersonal relationships. We believe that most people want to "Do unto others as you would have them do unto you." The management of this firm firmly supports this policy and will make every effort to ensure its implementation.

---

establishes the following standard: if the firm is to function most effectively, employees must respect each other's gender, race, religion, age, and so forth. They must know that any form of harassment is unacceptable. By having such a policy, a firm can communicate the importance it places on the notion of mutual respect.

The well-known retailer Wal-Mart has developed a harassment policy that is consistent with what we are advocating. It states, in part:

Harassment of any type whether sexual, ethnic, racial, etc., is not tolerated at Wal-Mart. We want to provide a work environment where everyone is comfortable. Harassment includes offensive language, gestures, physical contact or other conduct that destroys that environment. . . . Harassment of any type is inconsistent with Wal-Mart's belief in respect for the individual and will not be tolerated.

MANAGING OFFICE ROMANCES

Unlike harassment, consensual romantic relations between managers and their employees or between coworkers are not a violation of law. However, such behavior has the potential to create problems and disciplinary action may be required. Employees engaged in office romance may, for example, spend more time becoming acquainted with each other and less time concentrating on their jobs. In addition, it is not uncommon for consensual relationships to deteriorate into sexual harassment charges or create an atmosphere that is detrimental in terms of getting work done. In any event, dating, especially between supervisors and subordinates, is a veritable time bomb waiting to explode.

Many employers are finding that they have a legitimate interest in regulating office romances. Clearly, these relationships can have a significant effect on productivity. As a result, many corporations are seeing a need to develop coherent policies on such issues in order to reduce the risk of litigation, decreased morale, and reduced profits.[13]

Research on workplace affairs and romances shows the dilemma being faced more and more by American businesses: To what extent can an organization limit what seems to be a basic employee right? The workplace is a natural environment for the development of romantic relationships, because proximity is always a prime factor in affiliation. Indeed, liaisons are virtually unavoidable as men and women spend long hours on the job together. The workplace also provides an atmosphere wherein people come to know each other better. Familiarity and sharing of similar values and interests inevitably bring people together. In addition, the tension and excitement of working toward a common goal often generate mutual affinity.[14] Nonetheless, the bulk of the literature does not find positive relationships between office romances and effective work performance. Indeed, the reverse is usually the case.

What, then, should corporations do? Should they establish a strict policy prohibiting fraternization, or might it be better to accept the fact that affairs at work are inevitable? Because this is a gray area for corporate policy making that may truly conflict with the employees' legitimate right to privacy, managers have a broad range of attitudes and opinions on the subject. In fact, many find ways to dodge the question. "Office romance? I wouldn't touch it with a ten-foot pole!" is a typical response. Yet some firms have developed strategies to address the issue of office romances. Often these actions lead to specific disciplinary policies that attempt to define the ground rules and discourage or prohibit the relationships.[15] This is especially true when the affair involves a manager and one of his/her subordinates.

Corporate Responses to Office Romances

Many financial, insurance, and accounting firms (especially those with more conservative cultures) have developed formal rules or policies that discourage close working relationships between married or unmarried employees. For example, at Arthur Anderson and Company there is a strict rule that prohibits partners from marrying other employees. If this occurs, one member of the couple must leave. A similar policy has been adopted at Price Waterhouse. According to the Human Resource Managing Partner,

It is the policy of our firm to permit employment of relatives and staff members in the firm and in the same practice unit, except that a relative of a partner may not be employed in the same practice unit or geographic location. For the purposes of this policy, a relative is defined as a spouse, all dependent persons, and the following non-dependent persons and their spouses: child, brother, sister, parent, grandparent, or parent-in-law.[16]

Especially in financial firms, it makes sense to adopt strict policies against nepotism. Conflicts of interest may develop if the couple works in the same department. Highly confidential information could be compromised, and collusion could disrupt the integrity of the firm. At Connecticut Bank and Trust Company (CBT), a prominent bank in the Northeast, security reasons may prohibit married couples or relatives in the firm from working together. The CBT policy reads: "Employees related by blood or marriage are discouraged from working in the same area of the bank. Situations where relatives do work together in the same area will be reviewed."[17]

For a number of solid business reasons, many firms discourage or prohibit office relationships and romances. However, there is another issue here. As we noted earlier, relationships that begin as mutually consensual affairs often turn nasty and one of the parties feels exploited. In other cases one party seeks to end the relationship but the other person does not accept this, and charges of sexual harassment are the final outcome.

Despite this, some firms do openly support—or at least do not discourage—office romance. In these organizations relationships are believed to contribute to both morale and productivity. A vice president of personnel in a sports manufacturing firm has said, "In this company there is great respect for privacy. No one will pay much attention to this kind of problem because it is considered an issue of employee privacy." Apple Computer is another good example. According to the Human Resource Director, "We do not have a formal policy against romances among employees. We do not try to control or monitor these situations." Another Apple employee stated, "At Apple, there is an unspoken attitude that says that if you get involved with another person at Apple, that person will be aware of your work and sensitive to the demands and pressures of your work . . . so romancing in the office may even be good for business. Because people work so many long, hard hours around here, you also have few opportunities to meet anyone else. . . . The company benefits enormously when two employees are involved." Indeed, in firms such as Apple, office romances may even be unofficially encouraged as a means of reducing turnover and promoting productivity.[18]

No matter what the official policy of the organization, many executives have adopted a middle-of-the-road position. Because there are legitimate concerns regarding unwarranted invasion of employee privacy, they may prefer to let the romance run its course—as long as it doesn't affect business. The argument is that one's personal life is one's own private business. If the romance does affect business, the firms intervene quickly and decisively. This is particularly true whenever:[19]

- There is a direct reporting relationship between the parties;
- The parties are engaged in an extramarital affair;
- There is the potential for conflict of interest.

What actions do these firms take if the above conditions exist?[20] For minor offenses:

- Informal discussion and/or counseling for both members of the couple regarding the implications of their actions on the work group;
- Formal warning if performance is dropping;
- Participative discussions regarding transfers for one or both members of the couple if job performance remains adversely affected or if the work group continues to suffer.

For more severe offenses:

- Formal warnings and disclosure of the problems the romance has caused;
- Direct transfer of one party if a conflict of interest becomes evident or if exploitation is suspected;
- Termination if there is any reasonable certainty of a serious violation of workplace professionalism such as sex traded for promotion or engaging in sexual activities while at work. (As long as the firm is operating in good faith, various courts have rejected claims of wrongful discharge.)

USING OFFENSIVE OR ABUSIVE LANGUAGE

Another problem area related to improper interpersonal conduct occurs when employees (such as John Moore in the opening incident) use language that is unprofessional, vulgar, and possibly offensive. This can run the gamut from language that is really nothing more than very bad taste and shows a lack of sensitivity to others, to a situation that may constitute sexual, racial, or some other form of unlawful harassment. Of special note would be the case of *Holland v. First Virginia Banks* (discussed in Chapter 2) in which a black employee was bombarded with racial slurs delivered by his immediate supervisor.

Organizations typically address this issue with a short policy statement saying that such behavior will not be tolerated. For example, one shipbuilding firm states in its *Yard Regulations* that "abusive, obscene, immoral, or indecent language or behavior" is one of the acts and practices that are expressly prohibited. The City of Virginia Beach gives as an example of conduct that may require disciplinary action, "use of offensive, abusive, threatening, coercive, indecent, or discourteous language toward supervisors, other employees or the public." Finally, a large medical facility's policy states that "using profane or abusive language" may lead to termination.

Even when there are clear rules, before a manager can determine what disciplinary action (if any) is appropriate, a few basic issues must be considered. For example, to what extent is "rough" language an established, historical part of the workplace environment? Clearly, a traditional industrial organization such as a shipyard would be more tolerant than a white-collar professional firm such as a bank. Another issue involves whether the employees are dealing directly with the public and important clients. In a retail environment, employees must be very careful of language so as not to offend customers. Yet another issue involves the intent of the rough language. Is it being used in true jest among friends, or is it a device to intimidate, demean, and harass other employees such as women and minorities? In addition, how rough is the language? Are employees making constant reference to intimate body parts and sexual practices, or does someone just say "damn" more often than he/she should in a professional situation? The answers to these and other questions will allow the organization to respond in a way that is both fair and reasonable.

Generally, unless someone is likely to charge harassment, the firm should be able to treat the abusive or crude language as a minor offense and use verbal and written warnings to eliminate the problem. But if these sanctions do not work, or when the offense is much more serious, suspension or summary dismissal will be the proper disciplinary response.

This last point is illustrated by an arbitration case involving Engineering Air Systems, Inc.[21] The grievant and a fellow employee, upon arriving for the third shift, found the rear gate to the plant locked. In order to clock in they proceeded to the front door and rang the bell. The security officer who had locked the rear gate opened the front door. Upon entering, the grievant accused the guard of locking up prior to 11:00 P.M. When the officer denied this, an argument ensued. During the course of the heated discussion, the employee called the security guard several unprintable names. At this point the shop steward arrived and stepped between the two men. The grievant then picked up an 18-inch crescent wrench but did not swing it at anyone. As a result, the employee was suspended for three days without pay.

The grievant had a good work record; but even so, the arbitrator ruled that the suspension was appropriate. Because the employee had clearly violated a rule against profane and abusive language, it was felt that no mitigating circumstances could justify the grievant venting his rage in this manner.

CONCLUSION

If an organization is to operate effectively and maintain a favorable public image, its employees must behave in a manner that does not offend others or jeopardize the ability and willingness of people to work together effectively. Thus, for a variety of reasons organizations have an obligation to establish rules regarding interpersonal conduct.

In this chapter we have examined three forms of interpersonal conduct that can cause serious problems and can require disciplinary actions on the part of managers. Obscene or vulgar language used by one employee in the presence of others is probably the most common. Although this is not a simple matter, it is not an especially difficult problem. Much more complex and dangerous are situations in which someone is harassing another employee on the basis of that person's gender, race, ethnic background, or other status. Since the U.S. Supreme Court decision in *Meritor Savings Bank v. Vinson*, there has been a great deal of litigation; most firms should now understand that when harassment is severe enough to alter the conditions of employment, swift action must be taken. In between these two extremes is the everyday problem of workplace romances, which often lead to sticky situations down the road.

When deciding how to respond to these and other forms of improper interpersonal conduct, managers need to use good judgment and take actions that are sufficient to remedy the problem. Nevertheless, with the exception of harassment (which is clearly a violation of law), there are probably more legitimate employee privacy rights issues over sex-related activities than would be true for any other topic covered in this book. In short, there is a fine line between a sufficient remedy and managerial overreaction.

NOTES

1. J. L. Carbonell, J. Higginbotham, and J. Sample, "Sexual Harassment of Women in the Workforce: Managerial Strategies for Understanding, Preventing and Limiting Liability," in *The 1990 Annual: Developing Human Resources* (San Diego, CA: University Associates, 1990).

2. *Daily Press/Times Herald*, September 12, 1990.

3. L. Farley, *Sexual Shakedown: The Sexual Harassment of Women on the Job* (New York: McGraw-Hill, 1978).

4. C. Safran, "What Men Do to Women on the Job: A Shocking Look at Sexual Harassment," *Redbook*, November 1976.

5. P. J. Champagne and R. B. McAfee, "Auditing Sexual Harassment," *Personnel Journal*, June 1989.

6. Ibid.

7. Ibid.

8. Bureau of National Affairs, *Corporate Affairs: Nepotism, Office Romance, and Sexual Harassment* (Washington, DC: BNA, 1988).

9. A. F. Silbergeld, "Reasonable Victim Test for Judging Hostile Environment Sexual Harassment Cases," *Employment Relations Today*, Summer 1991.

10. Kruchko and Fries, *Employee Relations Newsletter*, December 1991.

11. Champagne and McAfee, "Auditing Sexual Harassment."

12. *Daily Press/Times Herald*, September 12, 1990.

13. C. J. Anderson and C. Fisher, "Male-Female Relationships in the Workplace: Perceived Motivations in Office Romance," *Sex Roles* 25, no. 314 (1991).

14. Ibid.

15. L. Mainiero, *Office Romance: Love, Power and Sex in the Workplace* (New York: Rawson Associates, 1989).

16. Ibid.

17. Ibid.

18. Ibid.

19. Ibid.

20. Ibid.

21. Engineering Air Systems, Inc., Labor Arbitration Awards, cited 86-2 ARB, 1986.

Chapter 9

Controlling Employee Horseplay, Assault, and Fighting

The warehouse of a large plant in St. Paul was divided into several sections with a different manager heading up each area. Joe Lewis was in charge of the Dismantling Department. Joe subscribed to the "Theory Y" style of management, and he usually gave employees considerable freedom and discretion in terms of their activities. Production from this section of the warehouse was continually higher than that of other departments. Joe's employees thought very highly of him; in fact, they considered him one of the gang.

One night, while on an overtime assignment, the workers in Joe's section started to play games—as they had frequently done in the past. But this time the game got out of hand; and before the shift was over, one of the workers had driven a forklift through one of the walls of the warehouse. When Joe saw the hole he immediately confronted the group. "Okay, who's been playing roller derby with the forklift?" Everyone stared and waited for someone to respond, but nobody answered.

What does one do in this situation? How should Joe proceed? Clearly the matter is serious, but nobody seems to have been injured. Yet company property has been damaged, and next time an injury could easily result.

Situations such as this happen all too often. Although management may be inclined to overlook a bit of horseplay, the behavior may escalate and fighting or assault can result. Aggressive action must be taken, but it is important not to overreact.

This chapter examines three common forms of disruptive employee behavior: horseplay, assault, and fighting. Alternative approaches for resolving these problems are presented along with typical company policies, legal considerations, and relevant arbitration cases.

HORSEPLAY

Horseplay has been defined as "rough or boisterous play that disrupts normal or routine functions." It is generally viewed as behavior that is essentially without malice but childish and infantile, resulting from "uncurbed impulses," "yielding once to such a temptation," or the "fallible nature of the human condition."[1] Of the three behavioral problems discussed in this chapter, it is the most common and the most difficult to assess and correct.

Because horseplay can get out of hand, most firms have policies that prohibit it. These policies are typically very short and simply state that there is to be "No horseplay." For example, one large hospital's policy states that "horseplay, scuffling, or throwing objects" will result in a written warning on the first offense. Likewise, a construction firm's policy states that employees should not participate in "games, scuffling, horseplay, unnecessary shouting, or deliberately creating a confusion on the premises." Some policies spell out the penalty given if a violation occurs, whereas others say only that violators will be subject to "disciplinary action."

Unfortunately, the term "horseplay" is not precisely defined in most of these policies, so employees and supervisors alike are often confused over which behaviors fall within it. Workers who are not familiar with the customs and culture of the United States may understand the term even less. As a result, managers may want to clarify this for employees, particularly if it is a problem.

When employees engage in horseplay, managers must decide what the appropriate penalty, if any, should be. Over the years arbitrators have been asked to rule on numerous cases, and their decisions provide valuable advice to managers.

Even though arbitrators generally argue that employers do have a right to expect reasonably social, adult behavior from employees, they recognize that some goofing around is inevitable. They recommend that before taking action a manager should determine the exact nature of the problem and not overreact but, rather, take disciplinary action that is appropriate.

Consider the case involving Southeast Container Corporation in which an employee was summarily discharged for smearing red paint on the handle of a press machine. The arbitrator held that this type of horseplay is a fact of industrial life and that the employee's actions were not so bad as to warrant bypassing the progressive penalty system. On the other hand, the arbitrator in the case of Monsanto Chemical Intermediaries Company took a somewhat different view. In this situation, two male employees were given a thirty-day suspension for locking a woman in a supply room and attempting to pull off her clothes. They argued that it was all a joke, but the arbitrator disagreed because their actions involved physical assault and the woman felt legitimately threatened.

In another case involving the Martin-Marietta Corporation, one employee who was driving a flatbed truck purposefully bumped into the back of a forklift driven by another worker. The truck driver then pushed the forklift for some 40 feet at a speed faster than its capacity. The forklift driver lost control and the back end of the forklift tilted at a 45-degree angle. Fearing the forklift would roll over, the driver jumped off. The forklift continued on and the driver eventually managed to retrieve it. Upon inspection, the flatbed truck was found to be in working order, with no brake fluid loss. In deciding whether the firm was justified in terminating the flatbed truck operator, the arbitrator stated that: "Safety in the workplace is a paramount concern of both employers and employees. Activities which are intended or which are likely to create the risk of serious harm cannot be countenanced." The arbitrator upheld the discharge and concluded that pushing the slower-moving forklift, knowing that it might go out of control, was inherently dangerous and that the potential for serious injury or death was obvious.[2]

Similarly, an arbitrator had to determine the severity of the offense in a horseplay case involving employees at Beatrice Meats, Inc.[3] One day a female employee who worked as a scaler tricked three coworkers into chewing a laxative form of chewing gum. Later, she told one of the employees about the prank and this employee told the others. Within hours, each employee experienced completely "freed" bowel movements. The firm then discharged the ten-year employee for horseplay.

In deciding the case, the arbitrator concluded that the employee's actions did not reflect a realistic threat to the safety of her coworkers or a danger to the firm's operations. It was a childish prank that reflected on the grievant's character but not her overall fitness to remain as an employee. It was not akin to physical assault, which would have justified discharge. The arbitrator reinstated the employee, but without pay for time lost.

Although these cases primarily focus on determining the severity of the offense, this is not the only factor that determines the appropriate penalty. Arbitrators also consider the employee's work record, length of service, past disciplinary record, and any mitigating circumstances surrounding the incident. For example, in an incident at Erwin Mills, Inc., one employee who had been needling a fellow worker all morning was, in retaliation, unexpectedly grabbed in a bearhug. In defense, the man drew a pocket knife and made a slicing motion, for which he was later discharged. The arbitrator reinstated the employee but without back pay, noting that he had a nearly perfect record of nineteen years' service.[4] In another case, an employee who had a history of vicious teasing picked up an empty wire spool and playfully tossed it at a female employee, hitting her in the thigh.

She wheeled around, grabbed the spool, and heaved it back nearly missing the head of another worker. The supervisor then fired both employees. The female employee appealed the decision and the arbitrator reinstated her without loss of seniority and with back pay, reasoning that because supervisors at the firm had known about this situation for some time and had done nothing, a measure of responsibility rested with the company. Thus, management's failure to consistently enforce its horseplay policy was the deciding factor.[5]

ASSAULT/BATTERY

Black's Law Dictionary defines assault as "any willful attempt or threat to inflict injury upon the person of another, when coupled with an apparent present ability so to do, and any intentional display of force such as would give the victim reason to fear or expect immediate bodily harm."[6] Assault is often accompanied by "battery." However, the two differ in that the latter requires physical contact (bodily injury or offensive touching), whereas the former can be committed without such contact. An assault and battery is both a tort and a crime. If an assault is committed with the intention of committing some additional crime or is attended with circumstances of peculiar outrage or atrocity, it is referred to as "aggravated assault."[7]

Company policies typically treat assault as a very serious offense. For example, one firm's policy states that employees will be fired on the first offense for "physical assault on employer or his representatives or other employees while on duty or on company property." Likewise, a large furniture store states that "threatened or actual physical violence toward a coworker or customer may result in suspension without pay for three days or, if warranted under the circumstances, discharge." A large hospital's policy states that "engaging in heated arguments" is unacceptable and will result in a written warning on the first offense. It adds that "committing an act of violence" will result in a suspension or termination on the first offense. Keep in mind that in addition to any penalty a firm might give, the victim of an assault and battery could also take legal action against the offender.

Some firms include in their assault policy a provision covering firearms. To illustrate, one clothing store states that "possession of weapons on company premises at any time unless specifically authorized by the Director of Loss Prevention" may be "cause for immediate termination." A large hospital's policy states that "possessing explosives, firearms, or dangerous weapons" will result in suspension or discharge on the first offense.

Arbitrators are frequently called upon to judge assault cases, and several unique issues surface when these cases are heard. One of these is determining whether an actual threat took place. For example, calling another a "dodo" and a "turkey" has not been considered a threat. However, when an employee told another that "Big Daddy will get you" if he didn't join the union, the arbitrator held that this constituted a threat because the employee could have reasonably believed he was being threatened. In another case, the arbitrator concluded that an employee's comment, "I hope your truck blows up," was intended as a threat, given the circumstances. Another issue that surfaces in threat cases involves whether they are accompanied by weapons. Threats made with weapons are viewed as more serious than those without. In one case, an employee with thirty years of service pulled a knife, held it to a fellow employee's stomach, and threatened to cut the employee to pieces. The arbitrator in the case sustained the discharge on account of the severity of the offense.[8]

One of the fastest growing crimes in the United States is workplace homicide in which a disgruntled present employee or former employee takes violent action against members of the firm. Consider the case of a technician who was discharged from Elgar Corporation, located in San Diego. Three months later, in June 1991, he returned wearing a bandoleer of ammunition around his chest and carrying a 12-gauge shotgun and a rifle. He shot out the plant's telephone network, detonated two radio bombs, and killed two executives. In another case a disgruntled female employee at the Eveready Battery plant in Bennington, Vermont, shot and killed the plant manager and critically wounded two others after trying to set fire to the plant. Finally, a post office employee who had been recently nominated for "letter carrier of the year" in Escondito, California, shot his wife and then went to work and killed two coworkers and later himself. The reason: he was enraged over a new rule prohibiting employees from smoking in their jeeps.

Although such incidents are rare, it behooves managers to be alert to the possibility and take appropriate action. When employees are furloughed, firms may want to give considerable forewarning (such as the sixty-day notice provided by General Dynamics). Workers terminated for cause could be given exit interviews by specialists to reduce their anger. Security guards should be notified which employees have been dismissed and told not to let them back in the facility. Furthermore, managers should be alert to warning signs, such as sudden behavioral changes, and should conduct discharge interviews in a nonconfrontational way. Grievance procedures that give employees a chance to be heard may also help.

FIGHTING

Fighting is defined by *Black's Law Dictionary* as a "hostile encounter; either physical or verbal in nature."[9] As with horseplay, most firms have a policy against it. These policies are typically very short. For example, one shipyard's policy states that "Fighting on Company Property" is "expressly prohibited and will subject the offending employee to discharge or other discipline." Similarly, a supermarket's policy states that "Employees shall not provoke or participate in a fight or engage in any violent act, or threaten, intimidate, interfere with, or attempt injury to anyone or engage in disorderly conduct. The penalty for any store employee for the first offense of this kind is discharge."

Many firms combine their fighting policy with ones on horseplay and assault: "Courteous conduct is required of all employees in their dealing with the public, their subordinates, or each other. Violence, fighting, horseplay, threatening, or interfering with other employees while on duty is prohibited." Similarly, a railroad's policy states:

Committing any of the following acts will result in immediate discharge and any other government or private action deemed necessary: Fighting, assaulting, detaining or physically abusing any employee or supervisor; threatening bodily harm or using abusive language; any conduct contrary to common decency or morality, including disorderly conduct, horseplay, or any willful act which endangers others.

Arbitrators have been asked to judge numerous fighting cases, and a key consideration is the seriousness of the offense. Consider an incident that took place at the Transportation Manufacturing Corporation.[10] Two employees, who were apparently friends and had a history of calling one another names and grabbing one another in martial arts fashion, ultimately got into a fight and were terminated. On the day of the incident, Mr. N greeted Mr. S by the words, "hey, fool." At the end of the shift N called S a "nigger"; S responded by calling N an "Oriental faggot." This led to an outright exchange of blows with N's glasses being broken and his face cut, requiring three to five stitches to close the wound below his right eye. In judging the seriousness of the offense the arbitrator considered (1) whether the conduct consisted of a single, thoughtless blow or a series of deliberate acts; (2) whether the blow was struck with a dangerous instrument, a clenched fist, or an open hand; (3) the effect of the employee's "breach of shop etiquette" on the morale, safety, and work habits of other employees; (4) whether the incident indicated that the employee had vicious tendencies, a serious emotional instability, or dangerous propensities toward such conduct.

In deciding the case, the arbitrator recognized that the employer has a responsibility to its employees to provide a safe workplace and has a legitimate interest in protecting its property. Nonetheless, he reduced the discharge of both employees to suspensions, but without any back pay. He based his decision upon the following facts:

1. Both employees appeared to be contrite and recognized the negative aspects of their behavior.

2. The fight caused no lasting injury to either man.

3. No instrument or weapon was used.

4. There was no attempt to do serious bodily harm by either worker.

5. The firm admitted that the two employees were good workers.

6. The employees indicated there was no malice between them and they could work together in a peaceful manner.

7. The firm's rule against fighting does not mandate discharge in all cases.

Thus, in every case involving fighting, managers, like arbitrators, need to judge the seriousness of the offense—and this is not an easy task. The considerations used by the arbitrator in the last case cited could be helpful in making this judgment.

As with other types of problem behavior, the penalties for fighting can be mitigated by various factors, including length of service, past work record, past disciplinary record, and the likelihood that the behavior will be repeated. In cases of fighting, some arbitrators attempt to determine who started it and whether one employee was truly acting in self-defense. Whether or not the person seems contrite and recognizes the mistake may make a difference in terms of the penalty. However, most firms do not tolerate fighting and few arbitrators will reduce a penalty of summary dismissal.

On occasion, arbitrators have been asked to determine whether a firm can take action against employees who fight off company premises. As a general rule, off-duty fights are outside of management's jurisdiction. However, there are exceptions—such as the case of one employee who violently assaulted another. Here the arbitrator noted that the attack occurred very near the plant at a place where other employees were known to be present and that it occurred during the scheduled workday. In addition, it stemmed from activities inside the plant and involved other employees. Overall, because it disrupted plant operations, morale, and efficiency, management properly took disciplinary action.[11]

Dealing with a Fight

Suppose that a manager arrives at work one morning and finds two workers fighting. Punches are being thrown and each person is trying to wrestle the other to the floor. Both employees are bigger and stronger than the manager, and no one else appears to be trying to stop the fight. What would one do in this situation?

Breaking Up the Fight

Clearly, firms have an obligation to maintain a safe and healthy work environment for all employees. In addition, they want to protect and preserve their own property. Thus, the first step in dealing with a fight is to break it up. Some firms recommend that managers do this by yelling at the fighters to stop. If this fails the manager is instructed to threaten the combatants with disciplinary action, particularly termination. If both approaches fail, security or the police are called. Unfortunately, they may not arrive quickly enough to prevent injuries.

Some firms recommend that equipment such as a water hose or a grease gun be used to break up a fight. If this is done, one must be sure that the equipment does not hurt anyone. Some have suggested the use of fire extinguishers, but these are potentially dangerous and should be avoided.

Another alternative is to get other supervisors to help break up the fight by pulling the combatants apart. The problem in this scenario is that one of them may get hurt. However, the risk can be reduced by waiting for the fighters to tire before stepping in. Of course, some managers may be so husky or respected that their mere presence will cause fighters to stop.

One of the most complex issues is whether a manager should ask one or more nonsupervisors to help. Again, the risk is that these people may get hurt and blame the manager. As a general rule it is probably best not to ask, but this depends upon the degree of risk involved versus the likelihood that one of the combatants may get hurt if the fight continues.

Separating the Combatants

Once a fight has ended, it is important to keep the combatants separated long enough to insure that a new fight doesn't start. The importance of this can be seen in the case of two television station technicians who got into a fight and were returned to their work area. A few hours later the fight resumed, and one employee ultimately shot and killed the other.

Some firms suggest that managers suspend the offenders for at least the rest of the day to cool off. Others require that managers send the employees to different buildings, parts of the plant, or offices and keep close track of them.

Conducting a Fight Investigation

Once the parties have been properly separated, an investigation into what transpired must be conducted. This involves talking not only to the fighters themselves but also to any witnesses. Witness testimony is particularly important because those involved in the fight often have radically different stories. Consider the Transportation Manufacturing Corporation case cited earlier. Mr. N claimed that Mr. S came to his desk and put his hands around his neck. N pushed S away, and then each pushed the other. S finally got N's head in a headlock grip and hit him several times in the face, causing his glasses to break. N claims he never hit S, although he did swing wildly at him several times. S's version of the story is completely different. He claims he had just walked over to N's desk when N hit him with his right hand. N then came at him "like a windmill," so he put N in a headlock and hit him three times with "medium punches" "just to control him."

In conducting the investigation, several issues must be addressed. It is important to know exactly what transpired during the fight. In addition, the events that led up to the fight can be examined to determine why it started and who the instigator was. Another concern is who threw the first punch. Some firms recommend that a determination be made regarding who was the primary aggressor during the fight. All these issues come into play in determining the appropriate disciplinary action.

The impact of the fight on the various individuals involved, either directly or indirectly, also should be examined. To what extent did the fighters sustain injuries? What effect did the fight have on the morale, safety, and work habits of other employees? Will the combatants be able to work amicably together in the future?

In addition, an important part of any investigation is to review the firm's policy regarding fighting to determine exactly what it says and whether specific disciplinary action is required. It is advisable to review penalties in past fighting incidents to ensure both consistency and fairness.

Taking Disciplinary Action

Finally, in determining the appropriate penalties, the manager should follow the guidelines we have suggested in Chapter 3. That is, base penalties on the employees' work record, past disciplinary record, length of service, mitigating circumstances, and severity of the offense. The arbitrator's guidelines for evaluating the severity of the offense outlined previously in the Transportation Manufacturing Company case should prove helpful.

DEALING WITH MEDICAL EMERGENCIES

Whenever employees engage in horseplay, fighting, or physical assault, there is a good chance that one or more persons will be injured to the point that immediate medical treatment is required. One hopes this does not go beyond simple first aid. But suppose that more extensive intervention is necessary. Will the members of the organization be able to respond appropriately?[12]

Serious medical emergencies are unforeseen, unique events. Because they cannot be predicted, every organization should develop a specific plan of action before anything actually happens. As a general rule, an organization has two options. It can employ personnel who have appropriate backgrounds and training (possibly in-house medical professionals), or it can rely on outside emergency medical staff to respond.

If training of current workers is the chosen alternative, these individuals will have to be given proper instruction in both cardiopulmonary resuscitation (CPR) and first aid for traumatic injury. Although CPR is a standardized procedure for any nonbreathing, pulseless victim, first aid training is a very broad topic. As a result, the best approach to such a course is one that is based on the needs of the organization. However, arranging tailor-made first aid classes may be difficult and the company may be forced to fall back on standardized courses available from organizations like the American Red Cross.

In some cases firms that opt for on-site training will want, for various reasons, to limit the number of employees directly involved and focus the effort. For example, the firm may want to develop a few "mini–rescue squads" or "plant emergency teams." This approach attempts to bring more sophisticated medical attention to a seriously injured person, thereby increasing the likelihood that the victim will be stabilized at the workplace while waiting for community rescue personnel.

Yet even with a focused effort, it is still important that every employee be trained to a minimum level. New employee orientations should include not only specific job obligations and duties but also general company emergency and safety procedures. In addition, all personnel can be instructed in appropriate medical responses, such as calling for help appropriately and using standard company emergency plans. Such training could be routinely conducted, as are other important events such as fire and evacuation drills.

Perhaps the optimal approach combines both these ideas. Large groups of employees should be trained to manage medical emergencies in the sense of checking for breathing, putting pressure on a wound, calling for assistance, and so on. At the same time, coworkers with more extensive training can be summoned to deal with the needs of the victim until professional medical personnel arrive. For smaller firms that wish to be prepared for medical emergencies, the minimum essentials involve training in the recognition of acute breathing problems, establishment of a designated plan, a coordinator, and a few people trained in both CPR and basic first aid.

LEGAL CONSIDERATIONS IN ASSAULT, FIGHTING, AND HORSEPLAY

When confronting fighting, assault, or horseplay, managers must take immediate and direct action because they are directly responsible for such actions by employees. In most states common law recognizes two causes for action if managers ignore these behaviors or fail to respond appropriately. The first of these concepts is known as "respondeat superior," the other is "negligent hiring/retention." In either case, the general principle is that an employer is legally obligated to protect the safety of all parties with whom an employee may come into contact as a result of normal work activities.[13]

The two doctrines are not mutually exclusive. For example, in the Florida case of *Sixty-Six, Inc. v. Finley*[14] the employer was charged under both doctrines. A hotel patron was shot and paralyzed by an on-duty security guard with a gun that the hotel operators had authorized him to carry. The jury awarded $377,003.55 in finding the hotel operators guilty under both respondeat superior and negligent hiring. It was determined that (1) the guard was acting within the scope of his employment, and (2) the operators were negligent because they were aware he had discharged his weapon on at least two previous occasions, was known to drink heavily while on duty, and was intoxicated at the time of the shooting. Thus, by allowing a guard to drink and carry a gun, the operators had failed to provide a safe place for their patrons.

Respondeat Superior

The doctrine of respondeat superior ("let the superior reply") can be traced back to ancient civilizations and is based on the master-servant relationship. The concept holds that because the servant (employee) is the master's (employer's) legitimate agent, the master is responsible for the servant's acts.

The key issue in determining an employer's liability under respondeat superior is whether or not the employee was acting within the scope of employment. Although this may seem to be a relatively straightforward concept, determining which actions do or do not fall within the scope of employment has proved very troublesome. As a general rule it may be said that the doctrine does not apply if the employee's actions have no real connection with the job and are purely personal. However, suppose that an employee who is driving home from work has a serious accident while deviating from his/her customary route to drop off a package for the employer. Is the employer liable for injuries caused to the persons and property involved?

To deal with such ambiguities, over the years the courts have developed the doctrine of time, place, and purpose. If the employee's harmful conduct occurred during normal working hours at a place considered appropriate for the job, and if it resulted from an act whose purpose was to serve the employer's interest, then there is a legal basis for holding the employer liable.[15]

Assume, for example, that a plant guard assaults another employee whom he believes to be a prowler. If the court decides that excessive force was used and that damages must be paid, the employer could be held liable under respondeat superior on the basis of time, place, and purpose.

But say that the same guard inflicts severe injuries because he believes that the other employee is having an affair with his wife. In this situation, even though the factors of time and place are present, the employee was acting on his own behalf and not the employer's. Thus, the employer would probably not be held liable. However, if the employer knew about the action and in some fashion indicated endorsement, then the firm could be liable because the act was ratified. If the employer failed to take severe action against the guard, the courts could construe this as ratification of the act.[16]

Finally, it is generally recognized that because horseplay is always outside the scope of employment, the employer is not vicariously liable. In addition, if the assault or horseplay involved the use of an unauthorized weapon, respondeat superior probably would not apply.

Negligent Hiring/Retention

Negligent hiring is a recently developed doctrine that holds that the employer becomes directly liable for employee conduct on the grounds that the employer failed to exercise reasonable care in hiring employees who prove to be a danger to others. The assumption is that the employer could have and should have foreseen the propensity to engage in harmful behavior and thus could have prevented it. With negligent retention the employer would be held liable for overlooking certain employee behaviors or failing to dismiss someone for assault, fighting, or dangerous horseplay. Thus, in either case the employer's own negligence is presumed to be the proximate (direct) cause of the injury suffered.

Whereas respondeat superior covers only the actions that occur within the scope of employment, negligent hiring may cover events that occur outside the scope of employment. Thus, it considerably broadens the grounds on which the employer can be held liable. This is one of the legal characteristics that is crucial in distinguishing the negligent hiring theory from that of respondeat superior.[17]

For example, if during shopping hours a male store detective mistakenly grabs a female employee he thinks is shoplifting and breaks her arm, there is a strong case for employer liability under respondeat superior because of the time (during working hours), place (company premises), and purpose (acting on employer's behalf). Now assume that the same two employees meet at work and have a date after working hours, during which the male breaks the female's arm while trying to force her to have sex with him. On the basis of these facts alone, it is doubtful that the female has a case against the employer under respondeat superior or on any other basis.

However, what if she discovers that when the man was hired, the employer was aware that he had assaulted other women whom he had met at work—but had hired him anyway without warning her and other female employees of possible danger? Now she has strong grounds for bringing suit under negligent hiring even though the act occurred outside the scope of employment. The charge would be that the employer was negligent in failing to exercise reasonable care in the hiring and retention of a dangerous employee.

For example, in a case from the District of Columbia (*Fleming v. Bronfin*),[18] a female customer of a supermarket was sexually assaulted after the store's delivery man delivered her groceries and received payment. She brought suit, charging among other things that the supermarket owners were responsible because the employee was acting within the scope of his employment. The court rejected this claim based on the fact that once the groceries had been delivered and paid for, the employee from that point on was acting on his own behalf and not that of his employers. However, the court did sustain a claim of damages and ruled that the owners were guilty of negligent hiring in selecting an unsafe employee because they had "employed him without references and with no investigation of his character; [and] that defendants knew the man was addicted to the use of vanilla extract as an intoxicating beverage and on a previous occasion had discharged him for getting drunk on vanilla extract."

As a general rule, courts have taken the position that when an employer hires an employee, it must exercise the care of a reasonably prudent person in selecting people. This means that a reasonable effort should be made to obtain complete information through reference/background checks and careful interviews. Nobody should be hired unless this information is available.[19]

However, employers can take encouragement from the fact that the courts seem unwilling to place an undue or unreasonable burden on screening and hiring procedures. Cases that have resulted in verdicts of guilty for the employer, and especially those in which large awards have been made, seem to have as a common denominator what can only be called grossly inept hiring practices. For example, a jury in Indiana found an employer guilty of negligent hiring and awarded $800,000 in damages to a female employee of a car rental firm who was assaulted by a coworker.[20] What appeared to influence the jury was testimony that the firm had made only the most cursory check of the man's background; had ignored obvious time gaps in prior employment, omissions, and inconsistencies on the application; had failed to follow up on an affirmative answer about convictions other than traffic violations; had failed to uncover a prison term for robbery and assault; was not aware that the man was on parole and under a pending rape charge at his previous place of work; and had ignored signs of violent tendencies such as verbal threats, drinking on duty, and carrying a weapon.

Admittedly, this case is extreme. However, it illustrates that organizations that get into trouble have generally engaged in practices that violate even the most elementary principles of good personnel procedures. Fortunately, adequate screening of applicants is not based on some absolute standard but should be in keeping with the job. The courts are not likely to hold the organization to the same investigative standard for the person who sells candy behind a counter as for a security guard who carries a gun. Jobs that expose both fellow employees and the public to a greater risk if the employee later engages in violence require a more detailed check of a job applicant's personal and work history.

CONCLUSION

Statistics indicate that violent crime in the United States has been rising at an alarming rate, so it is not surprising that firms are seeing increased incidents of assaults, fighting, and horseplay. Furthermore, the trend is forecast to continue into the future. Thus, firms and managers alike need to be prepared.

Firms can reduce the likelihood of these incidents occurring by thoroughly investigating each applicant's background. Once the person is hired, the assault, fighting, and horseplay rules need to be explained so the worker knows the penalties and the importance of the rules. Furthermore, managers should be aware of the personalities and temperaments of their subordinates and watch how employees interrelate. If two employees are unable to work together effectively, they may need to be separated before violence erupts.

In addition, managers should monitor worker teasing and hazing. If all employees appear to be enjoying this, there is considerable give and take, and no one is being singled out, then so be it. However, there is a difference between friendly kidding and remarks designed to embarrass, ridicule, and humiliate another. Managers may need to remind employees of the difference and make sure that everyone is treated with respect.

Likewise, managers should monitor practical jokes and those who play them. These have the potential to get out of hand because the person on the receiving end of the joke may be embarrassed and repay the giver. Again, the key is to see how workers are reacting to the jokes.

All three behaviors discussed in this chapter can involve actual or potential violent interaction between employees. They are, however, somewhat different and must be handled in various ways in terms of disciplinary action. For example, most organizations specifically prohibit fighting on company property and discharge employees who violate the rule. This is especially true if one employee physically assaults another or attacks his/her supervisor. On the other hand, even though participating in horseplay is prohibited by many firms, employees who do this may be disciplined but not dismissed unless the behavior has caused injury to others or employees have violated the law.

NOTES

1. J. R. Redeker, *Employee Discipline: Policies and Practices* (Washington, DC: Bureau of National Affairs, 1989).

2. Martin-Marietta Corp., 86-2 ARB 8519.

3. Beatrice Meats, Inc., 86-2 ARB 8560.

4. Erwin Mills, Inc., 51 LA 225.

5. 26 LA 688.

6. H. C. Black, *Black's Law Dictionary* (St. Paul, MN: West Publishing, 1979).

7. Ibid.

8. Redeker, *Employee Discipline.*

9. Black, *Black's Law Dictionary.*

10. Transportation Manufacturing Corp., 87-1 ARB 8070.

11. Victorian Instrument Co., 40 LA 435.

12. L. M. Starr and S. Waymaster, "Coping with Medical Emergencies in the Workplace," *Personnel Administrator*, October 1985, pp. 21–32.

13. M. S. Novit, "Employer Liability for Employee Misconduct: Two Common Law Doctrines," *Personnel*, January–February 1982, pp. 18–27.

14. *Sixty-Six, Inc. v. Finley*, 224 So. 2d 381 (1969).

15. Novit, "Employer Liability."

16. Ibid.

17. Ibid.

18. *Fleming v. Bronfin*, 80 A. 2d 915 (1951).

19. Novit, "Employer Liability."

20. Ibid.

Chapter 10

Managing Smoking, Gambling, Sleeping, and Appearance Problems

One day after a meeting at Howell Products, two new members of the Board of Directors decided they would stay for lunch. Their host, Ken Fleming, Cafeteria Manager, suggested they try the luncheon special, Salisbury steak. Since it looked good, they both selected it along with potatoes, a salad, and pie. Unfortunately, when they began to eat, one of the Board members found a piece of a cigarette butt in his mashed potatoes. The manager, obviously embarrassed, headed to the kitchen to find Ron Burke, who was responsible for making the mashed potatoes. As Ken walked into the kitchen, he did not see Ron so he headed for a group of employees in the corner who were on a break discussing possible trades in their fantasy football league. They said Ron had gone to the storeroom, so Ken walked down the corridor and saw Ron coming the other way. He looked very tired and his white shirt was wrinkled and filthy with food stains. He asked Ron if he knew how the cigarette butt had gotten into the mashed potatoes, because the firm's policy strictly prohibits smoking in the cafeteria and kitchen. Ron responded, "I haven't any idea."

In this case, we have a situation in which a manager has a legitimate reason to believe that some employee has been smoking in the cafeteria in violation of the firm's smoking policy. At this point, however, he has no evidence other than a cigarette butt, so what can he do? Should he meet with all cafeteria employees as a group to discuss the incident, or should the firm develop a new smoking policy to deal with the issue? There is also the issue of Ron's appearance and whether he was sleeping on the job. Furthermore, what about the employees involved in the fantasy football league? Is this gambling or not?

This chapter examines four different forms of dysfunctional employee behavior: smoking, gambling, sleeping on the job, and improper attire and appearance. We present an overview of each problem, provide examples of company policies, and suggest different approaches for addressing these behaviors.

SMOKING

The issue of employee smoking has taken on ever greater significance in recent years as more and more firms have implemented policies designed to limit or ban smoking on the job. In addition, most states and many local governmental groups now have laws addressing smoking in public places such as restaurants. Nonetheless, even though firms are moving toward greater restrictions on smoking, the debate goes on and questions about the rights of smokers/nonsmokers and the effects of sidestream smoke persist. In this section we look at the issues, review the costs of smoking from an organizational perspective, and examine company policies and actions that attempt to address the concerns of the various parties.

Overview

In 1964 U.S. Surgeon General Luther Terry published the first official report on the health consequences of smoking. During the next fifteen years the number of articles and studies linking cigarette smoking to an array of diseases increased from 6,000 to 30,000. Eventually, this body of evidence led the United States Congress to require health warnings on cigarette packs.[1] More recently, the 1986 report by U.S. Surgeon General C. Everett Koop on the serious health hazards of involuntary sidestream smoke has added fuel to the ongoing debate.

Beginning in the 1980s more and more firms began to consider banning or, more often, restricting smoking in offices and plants. In 1987 the Bureau of National Affairs (BNA) surveyed 623 large corporations and found that 54 percent of the respondents had adopted some type of plan to restrict employee smoking. This was an increase from the 36 percent reported in 1986.[2]

As a typical example, on July 1, 1985, the New England Telephone Company, which employed 27,374 persons at approximately 600 sites, announced a companywide policy restricting smoking. Beginning that September smoking was banned in conference rooms and classrooms and was restricted in cafeterias and lounges. On March 1, 1986, smoking was prohibited in all work areas, including individual offices. Smoking areas were designated in cafeterias, lounges, hallways, and restrooms. A fulltime field manager was appointed for eighteen months to enforce the new policy and its implementation. Free onsite smoking cessation classes were offered to all employees.[3]

In some ways, however, the announcement by USG Corporation in 1987 that it would fire any of its 1,500–2,000 smoking employees who failed to stop immediately brought matters to a head. Following the press reports and a barrage of criticism of the policy, the company pulled back and said that smokers who did not cease would not be arbitrarily fired; rather, USG would provide further counseling.

Even though the proposed policy was never fully implemented, it raised a variety of important legal questions. Could a firm prohibit smoking, not only onsite but also at home and off the job? Would a company be justified in hiring only nonsmokers or requiring smokers to either quit smoking or lose their jobs? What if employees were to claim that their "addiction" to smoking was a handicap protected by federal law? What about nonsmokers? Suppose an employee refused to work in the presence of smokers and claimed that having an adverse physical reaction to secondhand smoke was a handicap?[4]

As matters currently stand, the question of who is handicapped remains open. As to whether a firm can ban smoking onsite, the answer is absolutely yes. In addition, hiring only nonsmokers is probably acceptable as long as the firm does not discriminate against protected minority groups. But can an organization force smoking employees to stop altogether? As a general rule, many legal experts argue that they cannot because what workers do off site is normally not the legitimate concern of an employer; and had USG attempted to implement its policy as originally stated, there might have been a flood of wrongful discharge actions. In summary, the issues remain complex and debatable. What does seem clear is that employers can establish rules that include restrictions or bans on smoking while on the job.

Costs of Smoking to Organizations

Even though the statistical evidence is conflicting at times, it appears that there are a variety of costs associated with having smokers (and smoking) in the workplace. These costs come from increases in absenteeism, medical care, insurance premiums (health, disability, life, etc.), on-the-job lost time for informal breaks and the smoking ritual of lighting up, property damage, depreciation, and maintenance.[5]

When smoking in the workplace first became an issue, it was a health issue—specifically the health of the worker. Of concern to the employer was the fact that employees who smoke have higher levels of absenteeism, increased medical care needs leading to higher insurance premiums, earlier deaths, and more lost productivity than nonsmokers. For example, on average the smoking employee is absent 50 percent more often, uses health insurance 1.5 times more, has an accident rate twice as high, and takes more time per day in breaks. All this translates into higher costs simply because an employee smokes.

In addition, there are costs associated with the act of smoking at work. When employees smoke in the office or plant, the smoke causes damage to facilities and the employer is faced with the increased risk of fires and burns, extra cleaning and maintenance, and more air filtration. If smoking did not occur, these costs would be automatically reduced.

Finally, there is the adverse effect of smoke on the health of nonsmokers. According to the American Cancer Society, nonsmokers exposed to sidestream smoke face a significantly increased risk of lung cancer and a variety of debilitating respiratory and coronary problems. Again, this leads to absenteeism as well as increased health, life, and disability insurance claims.

Employer Courses of Action

In terms of dealing with smoking issues an employer may follow several courses of action. Based on an assessment of the particular situation, an organization can choose to do nothing, accommodate smokers, restrict smoking areas and times, adopt a strict no smoking policy, or hire only nonsmokers.[6]

Do Nothing

It is almost certainly the case that virtually every firm has some smokers mixed in and working with nonsmokers. As long as all parties respect each other and nobody feels offended, there may be no need to take action immediately.

However, even if nonsmokers do not find other employees' smoke to be offensive, all the costs already noted still must be considered. In addition, there may be a cost associated with customers and other visitors who prefer a smoke-free environment.

In today's world, we suggest that "doing nothing" is not a viable approach for most organizations. Even firms that have all nonsmoking employees now need to have policies in place in order to address future situations. Besides, it is increasingly difficult to get away with doing nothing, primarily because nonsmoking employees have begun banding together to achieve their perceived right to a smoke-free work environment.

Accommodate Nonsmokers

Once the employer has decided to "do something," a course of action that accommodates nonsmokers may be a reasonable first step. For example, accommodation may be achieved by improving ventilation and filtering systems, installing partitions between workers, obtaining pledges from smokers to refrain while around coworkers, or allowing those nonsmokers who are physically affected by smoke to transfer to another location or shift. Accommodation, in a sense, may be the least offensive course of action for those employers who are not yet committed to a smoke-free environment but who want to avoid conflict among employees.

Restrict Smoking Areas and Times

If accommodating nonsmokers is not enough, the next move may be to adopt a simple policy that restricts smoking to designated areas/times (e.g., smoking in restricted areas is prohibited and subject to disciplinary action), or the restrictions may be more specifically stated. For example, the employer could allow smoking in specifically marked lounges, areas of a cafeteria, outside of the building, or during specific times such as lunch or breaks. However, there are three potential problems with this approach.

First, if smokers have to leave their work area there can be a serious productivity loss, and in fact the number of breaks and "travel times" often increases. Second, lounges and cafeterias may have to be modified significantly to prevent sidestream pollution. Often these architectural changes are not even possible. Third, if the areas cannot be modified, nonsmokers may demand expensive duplicate facilities.

Adopt a No Smoking Policy

Instead of restricting smokers to certain places or times, the employer may choose a total ban. This may be only inside of a building, but it can also be anywhere onsite. The only real restriction on the employer is that except in particular situations (as with firefighters), it appears that smoking at home or off site cannot easily be prohibited. There is, however, disagreement among legal experts on this point.

This is a fairly drastic course of action but one that has become more and more popular in the past few years. It does require an adjustment period and may lead to some initial resistance. Therefore, it should be phased in over a period of several months. In addition, assistance or incentives to help smokers quit may have to be provided by the employer.

The potential problem in this scenario is that some employees may be unwilling (or unable) to quit within the time allowed. This may lead to violations of the policy and subsequent conflict and disciplinary action.

Hire Only Nonsmokers

The most extreme approach would be to hire only nonsmokers. Although this may solve the long-term problem, most firms that do this must also have a "no smoking on company property" policy for current employees and will need to make every effort to get smokers to kick the habit altogether. Furthermore, this policy may make it more difficult to recruit new employees for some jobs.

Hiring of nonsmokers appears to be acceptable to the courts only as long as there is no adverse impact or discrimination against groups protected by federal law. Invasion of privacy is another consideration; but as long as the policy is well published, this should not be a problem. Finally, as we noted earlier, some smokers have tried to argue that they are handicapped and therefore must be accommodated under federal or state law. However, we know of no successful cases. In fact, courts seem more willing to extend handicapped status to nonsmokers.

Summary

As the percentage of adults who smoke continues to decrease and as the evidence of serious health effects mounts, more firms are restricting or banning smoking. In this section we have attempted to provide a brief overview of the problem, offer relevant empirical data, and examine several possible courses of action. From a disciplinary perspective, violation of a smoking policy will probably not lead to immediate dismissal on the first offense. Rather, this is one situation in which the progressive penalty system can be used and employees are generally given at least a second chance.

GAMBLING

Gambling in the United States is a very popular activity. This is evidenced by the fact that in 1988 fully $241 billion was wagered, representing approximately $1,000 for every man, woman, and child. An estimated $32.3 billion of this was wagered illegally on sports ($20.7 billion), horses ($6.1 billion), and numbers ($5.5 billion). People bet an estimated $17.1 billion on lotteries, $17.6 billion on pari-mutuels, and $161.9 billion at casinos.[7]

Although most people who gamble do so only on occasion, for approximately 2 percent to 4 percent of adults (and at least an equal proportion of adolescents) gambling creates a variety of personal and social problems. At least half of these individuals can be diagnosed as pathological gamblers. In a random sample of New York State residents, 1.5 percent were found to be probable pathological gamblers and an additional 2.8 percent had gambling problems. Male gamblers outnumbered females two to one, and gambling was higher for alcoholics and other drug abusers, nonwhites, younger adults, and those with lower incomes.[8] Furthermore, these figures are expected to increase as more and more cities and states permit gambling and hold their own lotteries.

Gambling has been defined as follows:

the dealing, operating, carrying on, conducting, maintaining or exposing for pay of any game. Making a bet. To plan, or game, for money or other stake; hence to stake money or other thing of value on an uncertain event. It involves not only chance, but a hope of gaining something beyond the amount played. Gambling consists of a consideration, an element of chance, and a reward.[9]

This definition excludes games of chance wherein nothing is wagered because of a lack of any consideration and rewards.

Most firms prohibit gambling because it is against the law in most states and is viewed by some as immoral and contrary to biblical teachings. In addition, it reduces the time spent working, may lead to theft and other dishonest acts, and can result in friction between employees. Consider the case of a group of twenty kitchen employees at a suburban Detroit hospital who had a lottery pool and won the state's $2.3 million jackpot. The club treasurer collected $4 from each member in January and bought twenty tickets for each of four Wednesday night Super Lotto drawings that month. But when the jackpot reached $18 million on a Saturday, the treasurer bought an unscheduled round of tickets. The problem was that six members had not contributed an extra dollar by the time the drawing was held. So the club treasurer determined that none of them were entitled to a share of the winnings. This outraged the excluded members so much that they filed a lawsuit. Moreover, the hospital suffered because these events significantly reduced the camaraderie that the workers had once felt. Indeed, some employees actually stopped talking to each other.[10]

Company gambling policies are typically quite brief. For example, one hospital states, "Promotion of, or participation in gambling, lottery or any other game of chance on hospital property will result in a 3-day suspension on the first offense and termination on the second." Likewise, a discount clothing store's policy states that "participating in any organized game of chance, punishable by law, while on company property or on company time, may be cause for immediate termination." Finally, one communication firm's policy is more elaborate; it prohibits the following:

gambling in any form, including, but not limited to, participating in wagering, card playing for stakes, raffles, lotteries, pools, numbers or punch cards, or any wagering of money not covered by the foregoing, while on company premises. This prohibition applies not only to the sale or distribution of tickets in raffles, lotteries, or pools, etc., but also to the purchase of such tickets. This prohibition applies regardless of the sponsorship or the beneficiary of the gambling activity.

Some firms exclude various sport pools from their policy, either explicitly or implicitly, as long as they involve small sums of money, cause no friction among employees, and do not take time away from work. They view these as a way of building morale and improving teamwork. For example, the administrators, faculty, and staff at one community college have approved of an "Institute of Gridology" (a football pool) that invites people to "become members" each week, and the person whose predictions are most accurate is given a "grant" to do "further studies on fore-casting and probability analysis." At the end of the football season, a party is held so all participants can meet each other and further "grants" can be awarded. The pool reportedly has improved communication and mo-rale among all concerned.

Dealing with Gamblers

To effectively deal with gambling on the job, managers must monitor employees on a day-to-day basis. This means looking for evidence of gam-bling such as cards, poker chips, dice, small pieces of paper being passed between employees, workers talking frequently on the telephone, employ-ees reading each other's pay stubs, and used lottery tickets or numbers slips. This also means looking for signs that some workers are compulsive gamblers. Robert Custer, a pioneer in developing treatment for compul-sive gamblers, has noted that the disorder typically passes through three phases: the winning phase, the losing phase, and the desperation phase.[11]

Although not every gambler experiences the winning phase, it is char-acterized by enhanced self-esteem and self-image as the person takes pride in the winnings and brags to others. People in this stage view themselves as important and smart, even lucky. For them, gambling becomes a solu-tion to life's problems and a remedy for anxiety, boredom, depression, and other unpleasant emotional states. The amount and frequency of bet-ting typically increase progressively at this time in order for the person to obtain the desired effect, which is similar to what occurs in alcohol and drug dependency cases.

During this phase many people bring their gambling activities to work and organize sports pools, trips to the races or casinos, lottery pools, and so on. Their optimism, high energy level, and seeming good luck may make them popular and the kind of employee for whom others are willing to cover. These people may also take on a second job in order to obtain extra gambling money.

The losing phase begins with a loss that injures the gamblers' self-esteem. However, instead of cutting back they "chase losses" by increasing their bets, which ultimately leads to even bigger losses. During this period there are emotional ups and downs, but the trend is toward increasing debt and deterioration of functioning.

The desperation stage is characterized by bouts of uncontrolled irra-tional betting and increasing psychological and physical symptoms. Mood-iness, difficulty in concentrating, and stress-related illnesses are common. In addition, some gamblers may steal, be dishonest, or engage in forgery while at work, justifying their behavior as a temporary expedient until the next big win.[12]

When they are confronted with a compulsive gambler, managers may want to recommend that the person join Gamblers Anonymous. This nationwide organization has chapters in many cities and charges no fees or dues for membership. The organization believes that compulsive gamblers have a progressive illness that can be controlled but not cured, and it offers a twelve-step recovery program that stresses personal recovery through group unity.

Managers are also free to discipline employees who are caught gambling on company property. However, arbitrators have generally concluded that discharge for the first offense is too severe a penalty. Therefore, using the progressive penalty system is normally the approach to take. In addition, arbitrators recommend that firms communicate their policies beforehand and that no disciplinary action be taken unless substantial proof exists. For example, in one firm a group of supervisors entered a room and saw five employees standing around a table. One man was pocketing a pair of dice, another was holding money in both hands, and $1.75 was on the table. The managers immediately fired the employees for gambling, and they in turn filed a grievance. Upon reviewing the case, the arbitrator ruled that sufficient evidence existed that the man holding the dice and the one with the money in both hands were gambling. However, there was insufficient evidence that the others were guilty. Moreover, the arbitrator ruled that a discharge was too severe a penalty for a first offense of gambling of this nature, given the fact that the firm had not given notice concerning gambling in the plant.[13]

Arbitrators also recommend that firms be consistent in enforcing gambling policies. The problem in many cases is that management looks the other way and permits the practice to exist without taking action. Then, when it gets out of hand, management decides to crack down by taking harsh action, thereby setting an "example." This shocks employees because they view it as unfair and often results in grievances. Thus, arbitrators recommend that before cracking down, managers should warn employees that henceforth no gambling will be permitted. It is important to note that arbitrator decisions in several cases suggest that just because management has tolerated innocuous games of chance such as World Series pools and Thanksgiving turkey raffles, it is not precluded from cracking down on employees who are involved in more serious forms of gambling such as bookmaking or numbers operations.[14] Indeed, arbitrators have found that discharge is appropriate when the employee was connected with an organized gambling racket, engaged in gambling during working hours, and the activity had a demonstrable effect on employee productivity and morale.[15]

SLEEPING

In August 1988, the Nuclear Regulatory Commission fined the operator of Pennsylvania's Peach Bottom nuclear power plant $1.25 million because thirty-three reactor workers slept or were negligent on the job. In addition, fines ranging from $500 to $1,000 were levied against the thirty-three present and former reactor operators and three top-level managers were barred from working in "any operational position." Sleeping on the job was reportedly so common at the plant that on one occasion a shift superintendent and three of the four reactor operators all dozed at once.[16]

As this case suggests, sleeping on the job can be a serious problem; as a result, it is addressed in most firms' work rules. A typical policy simply says that "sleeping is prohibited." On the other hand, some firms extend their policy to include behaviors often associated with sleeping, thereby giving them greater ability to take disciplinary action. For example, one hospital's policy states that employees will receive three days of disciplinary time off for "sleeping, or the appearance of sleeping, on the job." Likewise, a shipyard states that "sleeping or relaxing in an inattentive posture (even though not actually asleep) when supposed to be working or attentive, will subject the offending employee to discharge or other discipline." Finally, one large conglomerate's policy addresses the issue of where the employee is found sleeping. The policy states, "sleeping at assigned work station (employees will normally be sent home for the remainder of the shift)" will result in a documented written warning. It adds that "sleeping away from assigned work station is considered serious enough to warrant immediate suspension and normally discharge."

Dealing with a Sleeping Employee

Assume that a manager sees an employee who appears to be sleeping. His head is on his desk and his eyes are closed. But is he actually asleep? Perhaps he is meditating, simply resting his strained eyes, engaged in prayer, trying to think through a tough problem with his eyes shut, or is temporarily unconscious. How should the manager proceed?

Taking Disciplinary Action

Arbitrators suggest that managers have sufficient proof of sleeping before disciplinary action is warranted, but there is no definitive list of behaviors that are used in making this determination. However, several cases shed light on the issue. In a case involving the John Deere Company, the arbitrator differentiated between sleeping and nodding off, which is characterized by having eyes closed, head nodding lower and lower, jerking up, and then nodding again. He contended that nodding off may or may not lead to actual sleeping, which is characterized by complete unconsciousness.[17]

In another case a supervisor passed by the door of an employee who had her head down on her arms on her workbench with her eyes closed. He stood in the doorway for a few minutes and noticed that she did not move. He called over two other supervisors and the three of them watched for a while. Because of this, the employee was fired. In her appeal the employee claimed that she was between jobs, felt lousy, and had visited the medical department the night before—and was definitely not asleep. The arbitrator ultimately ruled in the employee's favor based on the fact that the manager only observed from a distance and was not present when the employee started working again. The arbitrator reinstated the employee, prescribing a one-week layoff for not keeping busy as the appropriate penalty.[18]

In another case involving the Union Tank Car Company, an employee was observed by three supervisors lying on his back wearing a protective hood that concealed his head. He was motionless and breathing rhythmically. A bright light shining on his head was repeatedly blocked out and then unblocked, yet the employee did not respond. After watching the employee for four or five more minutes, one manager kicked the man's foot. He reacted in a startled manner and, upon removing his hood, it was apparent that his eyes were red and he behaved as if he had been sleeping. He was accused of sleeping but had no rebuttal until later, when he filed a grievance. The arbitrator hearing the case concluded that the firm was justified in terminating the employee:

the observations of the three company officials in this instance, based on their protracted opportunity to perceive the situation, their unique efforts to arouse the individual, their uniform recollection of their perceptions, and the absence of any bias that would suggest a "slant" in their testimony, entitles them to significantly greater weight than that afforded the grievant.[19]

Finally, an operator in the Ready-to-Eat Processing area of a Quaker Oats plant was suspended for sleeping and filed a grievance. The manager claimed that he noticed the employee sitting in a reclined position with his feet up on his tool chest and his eyes closed. He called out to the worker on two occasions and shook him twice before he awoke. The employee denied that he was asleep, claimed he never heard the supervisor call out his name, and said he responded immediately upon being grabbed once by his left shoulder. Upon investigation, the arbitrator learned that the employee was hard of hearing and was wearing ear plugs, and that the noise level in the plant was such that it was difficult to understand any conversation at close range. Furthermore, a third person reported seeing the grievant awake only a few minutes before the supervisor reported seeing him asleep. Given these facts, the arbitrator overturned the suspension, stating that the firm had failed to show "by the greater weight or clarity of the evidence that the disciplined employee was guilty."[20]

Proving that an employee is actually asleep is not the only issue of concern to arbitrators. They also examine the firm's work rules and policies to determine if the no sleeping policy has been communicated to workers and how uniformly or equitably it is enforced. In addition, they consider whether the employee's behavior presents any threat to the health and/or safety as well as the security of other workers and property; whether the employee is asleep at his/her work area as opposed to some other area of the plant; whether the employee's assigned tasks are getting done; and whether the employee's behavior is a result of an unexpected reaction to medications.[21]

When an employee falls asleep, most firms look to their sleeping policy to determine the appropriate response. However, at least one firm has argued that when a person is sleeping he/she is also "stealing time" and, hence, is subject to the discharge penalty usually associated with "theft and dishonesty." Is this appropriate?

The issue surfaced in the case of a packer who worked for Gateway Foods and was discharged. One evening, an employee who had been out celebrating a special family occasion prior to work went to the second floor of the building, entered a room, locked the door, and went to sleep. He admitted that he did this and that he intended to return to work without being discovered. When the firm learned that he had been sleeping, he was terminated for "stealing time," a breach of the firm's "dishonesty" rule. The arbitrator hearing the case concluded that it was clear that the employee was guilty of sleeping and that intentionally seeking out a safe haven to sleep is more serious than inadvertently falling asleep at one's duty station. However, he ruled that the employee's behavior did not constitute "dishonesty," because in industrial settings "sleeping on the job just does not equate with stealing, theft, lying, or dishonesty as these terms are commonly interpreted." Thus, the employee was guilty of sleeping, not stealing; and because the firm's sleeping policy prescribed a written warning on the first offense, this was the appropriate penalty.[22]

Dealing with Narcoleptic Employees

Some employees fall asleep intentionally or because of medication, but at least 200,000 people sleep because of an affliction known as narcolepsy.[23] Although its cause is unknown, genetics plays an important part: studies show that people with narcoleptic relatives are sixty times more likely to develop the disease.

Narcolepsy outwardly resembles normal sleep, but there is a significant difference. Normal sleep consists of two different phases, paradoxical sleep associated with rapid eye movements (REM) and nonrapid eye movement sleep (NREM). In normal individuals, NREM sleep always precedes REM sleep and usually lasts for approximately sixty minutes. On the other hand, people with narcolepsy have almost instantaneous REM sleep with no preceding phase of NREM sleep.

People with narcolepsy not only suffer from sleep attacks, but some also experience momentary paralysis associated with sudden emotional reactions such as mirth, anger, fear, or joy. The person's paralysis may be confined to the limbs or may be more widespread. For example, one narcoleptic machinist's mate in the navy was eating with some friends at a restaurant, and the next thing he knew he woke up with his head on a plate. Apparently his fellow workers had told jokes that made him laugh, and this led to his collapse. He also suffered from hallucinations, once believing that a figure was standing in the middle of the road, but when he stopped the car, nobody was there.[24]

Employees who fall asleep as a result of narcolepsy should be referred to physicians for medical treatment. Some apparently benefit from medications such as Ritalin or codeine.[25]

PROPER ATTIRE AND APPEARANCE

Most firms allow employees considerable freedom in choosing what to wear to work. However, they may restrict this freedom for three major reasons. The Occupational Safety and Health Act requires that employers provide employees with a safe and healthy work environment; thus, out of necessity firms may require that specific attire be worn (e.g., ear protection, eyeglasses, and respirators). In addition, some firms are subject to local or state ordinances that prescribe attire for health reasons (e.g., wearing hairnets while working around food). Finally, firms may specify appropriate attire for business reasons (e.g., the need to create a desired public image: theme parks such as Busch Gardens or Epcot expect employees to wear costumes because they are part of the "show").

Typically, a firm establishes a dress policy, communicates it to employees, and takes disciplinary action following the progressive penalty system if the policy is violated. These policies range from quite general to very specific. For example, one firm's policy states that "failure to maintain a reasonably neat appearance will result in a reprimand on the first offense and second offense, a three-day layoff on the third offense, a one-week layoff on the fourth offense, and possible discharge on subsequent offenses." Although this policy does not spell out specifically what employees can and should not wear, Exhibit 10.1 shows the policy of a hotel that does. Exhibit 10.2 shows a shipyard's detailed policy of required safety attire.

Taking Disciplinary Action

Generally, arbitrators have recognized that an employee can be discharged for poor personal appearance or grooming as long as the employer's policy is directly related either to employee health or safety or to a legitimate business interest such as a firm's image.[26] In other words, an employer cannot impose a dress code that is the result of an arbitrary

Exhibit 10.1
Hotel Appearance/Dress Code

Just as we take great pride in our Hotel and service, the same should apply to our cleanliness, grooming, and appearance.

Your hair is to be neatly trimmed, clean, and combed. For sanitary purposes, long hair must be pulled close to your head and secured. Mustaches may be worn if they are full, neatly trimmed, and grown during a vacation. Men must be clean shaven and no beards are permitted.

Excessive jewelry and makeup should be avoided. Fingernails should be neatly manicured and cleaned and kept at a moderate length.

Daily baths or showers and the use of deodorants are important for your personal health and to avoid offending fellow employees and guests.

Non-uniformed employees are expected to dress in appropriate business attire, reflecting neatness, moderation, and professionalism.

Your manager has the right to send you home without pay to change if your appearance does not meet with approval.

---

decision based on personal taste. For example, in the case of Oxford Nursing Home, the employer had for twenty years maintained the same dress code requiring female employees to wear white dresses, shoes, and stockings. The women on staff filed a grievance requesting that they be allowed to wear white pantsuits. The arbitrator sustained the grievance, stating that the employer's dress code was an unreasonable exercise of management rights. He further noted that pantsuits were acceptable in many medical facilities and that the employer should keep up with the times.[27]

In reviewing discipline cases involving personal appearance and attire, most arbitrators first consider whether the rule is reasonably related to the employer's articulated purpose and then decide if it is consistently applied. If the rule seems reasonable, arbitrators are willing to disallow disciplinary action if the employee later conformed to the standard, had a legitimate reason for initially refusing to comply, or when years of service or work history entitled him/her to a second chance.[28] For example, in the case of Allied Chemical Corporation an employee was twice suspended and then discharged for refusing to comply with a newly enacted no beard policy for all employees using respirators. Following the notice of discharge, he relented and agreed to shave. The arbitrator ordered reinstatement based on the employee's fourteen years of service and his present willingness to conform to the rule.[29] Similarly, an employee working for Safeway Stores was fired for refusing to shave after a no beard rule went into effect. The man had worked at Safeway for five years and had always had a beard. He claimed that he should be exempt from the

Exhibit 10.2
Safety Attire Policy

---

1. Eye protection must be worn by all employees while in the yard, on vessels, and on down-the-river work.

2. Employees are required to dress safely for their work. Tennis shoes and sneakers are not permitted except for yacht work. Shirts must be worn at all times. Long hair must be secured behind the head or by hair net while exposed to the hazards of machinery and fire. Heavy-duty hair nets are available for this purpose. Hair styles, sideburns, or beards that interfere with the proper use of safety hats and respirators must be modified to afford the necessary protection.

3. Safety hats must be worn by all employees. Likewise, safety shoes must be worn on the job.

4. Respirators must be worn when working around fumes and dusts. Ask if you are not sure so you will have the correct respirator.

5. Approved ear protection must be worn in all areas where noise is a hazard. Ear plugs are available, as are ear muffs.

6. Safety belts must be used when working aloft and safety rails aren't available.

7. Use personal protective equipment such as aprons, goggles, face shields, and neoprene gloves when handling acids.

8. Protective gloves should be used when your hands are in contact with cleaning solvents, oils, and acids.

---

new rule because of a medically documented skin condition that made shaving extremely difficult. The arbitrator ruled that the company's rule must be followed because it was directly related to an attempt to present a certain public image and to compete for its market share of the retail food business. At the same time, however, the penalty was reduced to a leave of absence because given the employee's medical condition, discharge was too harsh.[30]

In the area of health and safety, an employer's dress or grooming code must be directly related to these concerns. In the Allied Chemical situation, for example, the arbitrator found that the no beard policy for all employees was not reasonable. It was acceptable, however, to apply the rule to those using respirators because facial hair could obstruct the seal and reduce the equipment's effectiveness. It is also generally agreed that employers can restrict certain types of clothing when employees are required to operate machinery, as long as protection of the employee is the rule's true purpose. Wearing of beards, finger rings, and wigs can also be banned. For example, hospitals can require certain dress for use in operating rooms for health and safety reasons.[31]

Even though the right to regulate the dress and appearance of employees is an established principle, one point is not entirely clear. Who bears the burden of proof where the reasonableness of the rule is at issue? On this, arbitrators disagree. On the one hand, as long as the employer can demonstrate that its standard applies to employees who have public contact and that it is attempting to project a given image for competitive business reasons, many arbitrators uphold the rule and the disciplinary action applied to employees who fail to comply.[32] For example, in a case involving Blue Cross of Northern California, the arbitrator upheld the firm's right to enforce a dress code without requiring the company to prove a relationship between dress code and public image.[33] On the other hand, the arbitrator's actions at Big Star No. 35 and Pacific Southwest Airlines required that the employers show a reasonable business necessity that a no beard rule had a rational connection with the operation of the business. Without this, the employers could not arbitrarily restrict their employees' right to determine their own personal appearance.[34]

In summary, there are several key points to remember in terms of rules for personal appearance and attire. First, the dress and grooming code must be reasonably related to workplace health and safety or to some legitimate business necessity. Second, the employee must be given actual or constructive notice of a dress or grooming code prior to the taking of disciplinary action. Third, the penalty must be consistent with the existing labor contract. Fourth, the policy must be uniformly applied and enforced.[35]

CONCLUSION

This chapter has examined four different forms of dysfunctional behavior: smoking, gambling, sleeping on the job, and improper attire and appearance. Each of these present unique problems for managers that need to be addressed and resolved. Each is different from the others, but there are similarities.

Smoking in the workplace has become an increasingly important topic because nonsmokers are becoming more adamant about protecting themselves from secondhand smoke, and they expect firms to establish policies that protect them. In response, companies are re-examining their policies and establishing new ones. As the number of smokers continues to decrease and laws change, more and more firms are likely to ban smoking from company property altogether.

Employee gambling is similar to smoking in that it can cause friction among workers. In addition, just as some people are addicted to cigarettes, others are compulsive gamblers. Firms often address both problems by referring afflicted employees to professional help or treatment centers. Beyond this, most firms develop policies to discourage both types of dysfunctional behavior and take progressive disciplinary action against violators.

In contrast, sleeping on the job and wearing improper attire usually do not cause friction among employees and do not involve an addiction; and managers rarely refer people who violate these rules for professional counseling. Rather, people typically sleep at work and wear unsatisfactory apparel on purpose, and the friction created is between the employee and the immediate supervisor. Nonetheless, most firms establish policies that regulate attire and prohibit sleeping at work. Offenders are usually disciplined according to the progressive penalty system.

NOTES

1. E. Fry, "Not Smoking in the Workplace: The Real Issue," *Business Horizons*, November–December 1990.

2. J. Nixon and J. West, "The Ethics of Smoking Policies," *Journal of Business Ethics* 8 (1989).

3. G. Sorensen et al., "Effects of a Worksite Nonsmoking Policy: Evidence for Increased Cessation," *American Journal of Public Health*, February 1991.

4. *Resource* (Society for Human Resource Management), March 1987.

5. Fry, "Not Smoking in the Workplace."

6. Ibid.

7. "America's Gambling Fever," *Business Week*, April 24, 1989, pp. 112–120.

8. S. B. Blume, "Compulsive Gambling," *Employee Assistance*, May 1991, pp. 10–12.

9. H. C. Black, *Black's Law Dictionary* (St. Paul, MN: West Publishing, 1979).

10. "Attempts to Divide $2.3 Million Split Friendships in Lottery Club," *Detroit Free Press*, March 6, 1988.

11. Blume, "Compulsive Gambling."

12. Ibid.

13. 28 LA 97.

14. 33 LA 175; 22 LA 210.

15. 45 LA 945; 17 LA 150; 13 LA 253.

16. "NRC Fines Firm $1.25 Million," *Detroit News*, August 12, 1988.

17. John Deere, Ottumwa Works, 27 LA 572.

18. 27 LA 137.

19. Union Tank Car Co., 89-2 ARB 8452.

20. The Quaker Oats Co., 89-2 ARB 8587.

21. A. E. Berkeley, "Asleep at the Wheel: How Arbitrators View Sleeping on the Job," *Arbitration Journal*, June 1991, pp. 48–51.

22. Gateway Foods, 89-2 ARB 8588.

23. *Newsweek*, July 13, 1981, p. 51.

24. Ibid.

25. J. Graedon, "New approaches may offer help for sufferers of narcolepsy," *The Virginian-Pilot and The Ledger-Star*, February 12, 1989, p. E2.

26. J. Redeker, *Employee Discipline: Policies and Practices* (Washington, DC: Bureau of National Affairs, 1989).

27. Oxford Nursing Home, 75 LA 1300.
28. Redeker, *Employee Discipline: Policies and Practices.*
29. Allied Chemical Corp., 76 LA 923.
30. Safeway Stores, 75 LA 798.
31. Redeker, *Employee Discipline: Policies and Practices.*
32. Ibid.
33. Blue Cross of Northern California, 73 LA 352.
34. Big Star No. 35, 73 LA 850; Pacific Southwest Airlines (Jones), 77 LA 320.
35. Redeker, *Employee Discipline: Policies and Practices.*

Index

About the Authors

R. BRUCE McAFEE is a Professor of Management at Old Dominion University. He has authored numerous articles and books, including *Motivating Strategies for Performance and Productivity* (Quorum Books, 1989) and *Organizational Behavior: A Manager's View*. He has conducted over 50 workshops on dealing with difficult employees, motivation, and leadership.

PAUL J. CHAMPAGNE, Professor of Management at Old Dominion University, has authored many articles in scholarly and practical journals. He is co-author of *Motivating Strategies for Performance and Productivity* (Quorum Books, 1989) and *Organizational Behavior: A Manager's View*. He consults with firms on an array of human resource matters including labor certification and equal employment opportunity.